FEEDBACK BLUEPRINT

UNLOCKING THE POWER OF CONSTRUCTIVE INSIGHTS

A COACHING CORNER SERIES

"Dr. Tenia's bold new book is a breath of fresh air for leaders that are driven to improve their company culture."
-Los Angeles Tribune Magazine

"The Feedback Blueprint is both brilliant and applicable to many more areas of life than just business."
-New York City Independent

net worlding
PUBLISHING

TENIA DAVIS, PHD

Book Design by HMDPUBLISHING

Net worlding
PUBLISHING

Library of Congress Control Number: 2024918554

THANK YOU

Thank you for embarking on this journey with me by choosing to delve into the pages of my book. As someone deeply passionate about the transformative power of feedback, I am thrilled to share insights and strategies aimed at enhancing your leadership prowess in this vital domain. Through these pages, my intention is to equip you with the tools and perspectives necessary to harness your full potential from constructive insights (feedback), which will allow you to grow and foster excellence in yourself as well as in those you lead.

Welcome to a journey of discovery, reflection, and empowered leadership.

Dr. Tenia Davis

CONTENTS

Welcome to the Coaching Corner

Welcome to "The Coaching Corner," a space dedicated to the ongoing development of leaders at all levels. In the dynamic and ever-evolving landscape of leadership, the pursuit of continuous learning stands as a cornerstone for success. This book is not just a collection of insights and strategies; it is a manifestation of a profound belief in the transformative power of continuous learning and growth.

As a seasoned Human Resources practitioner and academic researcher, I have dedicated my career to the art and science of leadership development. My journey has taken me through the corridors of various organizations, where I have witnessed firsthand the impact of effective leadership on teams and the broader business environment. This experience, coupled with rigorous academic research, has shaped my understanding of what it takes to nurture and develop leaders who are not only competent but also resilient, adaptable, and visionary.

The Coaching Corner is born out of my passion for developing leaders who can navigate the complexities of today's world with confidence and clarity. In an era where change is the only constant, leaders must embrace a mindset of lifelong learning. This book is designed to be your companion on this journey, offering practical tools, reflective exercises, and real-world examples to help you refine your leadership skills and foster a culture of continuous improvement within your organization.

Understanding the Coaching Corner Concept

The Coaching Corner concept is a multifaceted approach to leadership development, anchored in the belief that effective leadership arises from a commitment to continuous personal and professional growth. At its core, the Coaching Corner is both a physical and metaphorical space where leaders can engage in reflective practice, receive feedback, and hone their skills in a supportive environment. In *The Coaching Corner*, you will find:

A Space for Reflection and Learning: The Coaching Corner provides leaders with a dedicated space to step back from the hustle and bustle of daily operations and engage in meaningful reflection. This reflective practice is essential for gaining insights into one's leadership style, identifying areas for improvement, and setting actionable goals. By fostering a habit of regular reflection, leaders can develop a deeper understanding of their strengths and weaknesses, which is crucial for personal growth.

A Hub for Feedback and Dialogue: Central to the Coaching Corner is the emphasis on constructive feedback and open dialogue. Leaders are encouraged to seek feedback from peers, mentors, and team members to gain diverse perspectives on their performance. This feedback loop not only enhances self-awareness but also promotes a culture of transparency and continuous improvement within the organization. Open dialogue allows for the exchange of ideas, challenges, and solutions, enriching the leader's experience and broadening their horizons.

A Laboratory for Experimentation and Innovation: The Coaching Corner is a safe space for leaders to experiment with new ideas, strategies, and approaches without the fear of failure. By fostering an environment that encourages innovation and calculated risk-taking, leaders can push the boundaries of conventional thinking and explore creative solutions to complex problems. This experimental mindset is essential for staying agile and adaptable in a rapidly changing world.

A Sanctuary for Support and Encouragement: Leadership can be a lonely journey, filled with challenges and uncertainties. The Coaching Corner offers a sanctuary where leaders can find support and encouragement from like-minded individuals. This community aspect is vital for sustaining motivation and resilience. By connecting with others who share similar goals and challenges, leaders can draw strength from collective wisdom and experience.

A Platform for Skill Development and Mastery: The Coaching Corner is designed to provide leaders with the tools and resources needed to develop and master essential leadership skills. Through targeted training sessions, workshops, and coaching programs, leaders can enhance their competencies in areas such as communication, emotional intelligence, strategic thinking, and team management. This continuous skill development is critical for staying relevant and effective in an ever-evolving leadership landscape.

The Importance of Continuous Learning for Leaders

In today's fast-paced world, the only constant is change. Leaders who rest on their laurels and rely solely on past successes are likely to find themselves quickly outpaced by those who embrace a mindset of continuous learning. Continuous learning equips leaders with the ability to adapt to new challenges, innovate in the face of uncertainty, and inspire their teams to achieve extraordinary results.

Moreover, continuous learning fosters a growth mindset, characterized by a belief in the potential for development and improvement. Leaders with a growth mindset are more resilient, better able to navigate setbacks, and more likely to inspire and empower their teams. By committing to lifelong learning, leaders can cultivate a culture of curiosity and excellence within their organizations, driving sustained success and growth.

My Passion for Developing Leaders

My passion for developing leaders is rooted in a deep conviction that effective leadership is the key to unlocking the full potential of individuals and organizations. As a Human Resources practitioner and academic researcher, I have dedicated my career to understanding the nuances of leadership and exploring innovative approaches to leadership development. This book is a culmination of years of experience, research, and a heartfelt commitment to helping leaders thrive.

Through The Coaching Corner, I aim to share the insights, strategies, and tools that have proven effective in my work with leaders across various industries. My hope is that this book will serve as a valuable resource for leaders at all stages of their journey, providing them with the guidance and support needed to navigate the complexities of leadership with confidence and clarity.

Conclusion

Leadership is not a destination; it is a continuous journey of growth and self-discovery. Through the pages of this book, I invite you to explore the myriad dimensions of effective leadership, from self-awareness and emotional intelligence to strategic thinking and team empowerment. Each chapter is crafted to provide you with actionable insights and strategies that you can implement immediately, regardless of where you are in your leadership journey.

The Coaching Corner is more than a guide; it is a community of like-minded individuals committed to personal and professional development. You can find your community through following me at @theleadershipwise on Instagram. My website is theleadershipwise.com. As you embark on this journey, remember that the path to exceptional leadership is paved with curiosity, reflection, and a relentless pursuit of excellence. Together, we will explore the depths of leadership potential and unlock the capabilities that lie within each of us.

Thank you for joining me in The Coaching Corner. Let us embark on this transformative journey together, committed to the continuous development of our leadership abilities and the creation of a better, more inspiring future for all.

INTRODUCTION

Feedback is the cornerstone of effective communication, as a guiding light illuminating the path toward personal and professional growth. It is more than just a mere exchange of information; feedback is a dynamic process that shapes behavior, drives improvement, and fosters meaningful connections. In this chapter, we delve into the essence of feedback, exploring its definition, purpose, and significance in various spheres of life.

As a Human Resources executive with over 20 years of experience, I see leaders need help giving feedback to their staff and peers. It is one of the most challenging aspects of managing in the workplace. When delivered effectively, constructive feedback can lead to remarkable improvements in employee performance and overall team dynamics. Conversely, poor feedback can have crippling effects on company culture, leading to disengagement and reduced productivity.

My intention with this book is to provide a comprehensive blueprint for delivering feedback that fosters growth and development. It aims to equip leaders at all levels with the skills necessary to help their teams flourish. Effective feedback is crucial for individual growth and a positive and inclusive work environment.

Adding to the complexity, today's workforce spans five generations, each with unique work styles, communication preferences, and needs. Understanding and addressing these differences is essential for creating a sense of value, inclusivity, and belonging among all employees.

To bring these concepts to life, I have compiled stories from real experiences of many human resources practitioners. These stories serve as teachable moments, offering practical examples of behaviors and solutions that can help everyone develop their feedback skills. With practice, leaders can strengthen their ability to provide constructive feedback and become more confident in this critical aspect of leadership.

FEEDBACK STYLE MATTERS

In my career as an HR executive, I've encountered numerous leaders who struggled with the art of giving feedback. One leader, whom I'll refer to as Leader A, had a significant impact on their team—unfortunately, not in a positive way. Leader A was technically skilled and highly driven, but their approach to feedback was blunt and often perceived as harsh. They believed that being blunt, even to the point of being abrasive, was the best way to drive results.

NEGATIVE FEEDBACK STYLE

Leader A's feedback sessions were often one-sided, focusing solely on what employees did wrong, with little acknowledgment of their efforts or successes. This created an environment of fear and anxiety. Team members hesitated to speak up, share ideas, or ask for help, fearing negative criticism. Over time, this led to a decline in morale and a sense of distrust within the team. Productivity dropped, and turnover rates increased as employees sought more supportive work environments.

The repercussions of Leader A's feedback style extended beyond their immediate team. Other departments noticed the tension and discontent, which affected cross-functional collaborations. The overall company culture took a hit, becoming more siloed and less innovative. It was a stark reminder of how powerful feedback, when mishandled, can be in shaping—or dismantling—a company's culture.

CONSTRUCTIVE INSIGHTS AS A FEEDBACK STYLE

In contrast, I had the pleasure of working with another leader, Leader B, whose approach to feedback was exemplary. Leader B understood feedback is about pointing out mistakes, recognizing achievements, and guiding employees toward growth. Their feedback sessions were balanced, constructive, and delivered with empathy.

Leader B always began feedback sessions by highlighting what the employee was doing well, which helped to build confidence and trust. They then addressed areas for improvement with specific, actionable suggestions and always framed it in a way that showed their belief in the employee's potential to grow. Leader B also encouraged a two-way dialogue, allowing employees to express their thoughts and concerns, making them feel valued and heard.

This approach had a profound impact on the team's dynamics. Employees felt supported and motivated to take on challenges, knowing they had a leader invested in their development. The team thrived, showing higher engagement, creativity, and collaboration. This positive atmosphere was infectious, spreading to other teams and contributing to a more cohesive and innovative company culture.

The success of Leader B's approach was evident in improved performance metrics and employee satisfaction and retention rates. The company saw a marked improvement in morale and a renewed sense of unity and purpose.

BENEFITS OF CONSTRUCTIVE INSIGHTS

These contrasting stories highlight the critical role feedback plays in shaping company culture. Leader A's experience is a cautionary tale of the damage that poor feedback can inflict, while Leader B's success story demonstrates the transformative power of constructive, empathetic feedback.

As leaders, we must develop our feedback skills and approach this task to foster growth and trust. Doing so can create a work environment where employees feel valued, supported, and motivated to contribute their best. This, in turn, leads to a healthier, more vibrant company culture that benefits everyone.

CONSTRUCTIVE INSIGHTS VS. FEEDBACK:

Constructive Insights

Constructive insights are observations and interpretations designed to understand behaviors, situations, or outcomes better. They aim to inspire reflection, self-awareness, and new ways of thinking. Unlike direct feedback, insights are often shared through dialogue, exploratory questions, and storytelling, encouraging individuals to see things from a broader perspective. This approach helps individuals understand how their actions fit into the larger context, promoting long-term growth and innovation.

Feedback

Conversely, feedback is direct information given to individuals about their specific behaviors or performance. Its primary purpose is to reinforce positive actions and correct negative ones through clear, actionable suggestions. Effective feedback is timely, specific, and balanced, ensuring that individuals know exactly what is being addressed and how they can improve. This direct communication style helps drive immediate improvements and reinforces desired behaviors, contributing to overall productivity and performance.

Comparison

While constructive insights and feedback are essential for leadership and personal development, they serve different purposes. Constructive insights are also broad and inspirational, fostering self-awareness and long-term growth. Feedback is specific and actionable, focusing on immediate behavior changes. By understanding and effectively using both approaches, leaders can better develop their teams, create a positive work environment, and drive organizational success.

CONSTRUCTIVE INSIGHTS FRAMEWORK

CONSTRUCTIVE INSIGHTS

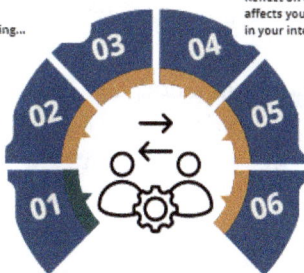

3. IMPACT
Explain the Impact.
This caused frustration and disrupted the flow of the meeting...

4. SELF AWARENESS
Foster understanding of one's own actions.
Reflect on how your communication style affects your colleagues. Are there any patterns in your interactions that could be improved?

2. BEHAVIOR
Specify Behavior.
You interrupted several times while others were speaking...

5. REFLECTION
Encourage recipient to reflect and respond.
How do you feel about this feedback? Do you have any additional thoughts?

1. SITUATION
Describe the Context.
During the team meeting on Monday...

6. NEXT STEPS
Provide actionable suggestions.
Next time, please wait until the person has finished speaking...

In today's fast-paced work environment, effective communication and constructive feedback are crucial for fostering a positive and productive workplace. The Enhanced Constructive

Insights Framework with Reflection and Self-Awareness provides a structured approach to giving and receiving feedback that not only addresses immediate concerns but also promotes long-term personal and professional growth. This framework consists of six key components: Situation, Behavior, Impact, Next Steps, Reflection, and Self-Awareness. Each component plays a vital role in ensuring that feedback is clear, actionable, and conducive to continuous improvement. By incorporating reflection and self-awareness, this framework goes beyond traditional feedback methods to encourage deeper introspection and understanding, ultimately leading to more mindful and effective leadership.

The Enhanced Constructive Insights Framework with Reflection and Self-Awareness is a comprehensive tool designed to enhance the effectiveness of feedback in the workplace. The framework's components—Situation, Behavior, Impact, Self-Awareness, Reflection, and Next Steps, —work together to provide a holistic approach to feedback. By clearly describing the context (Situation) and specifying the observed behavior (Behavior), the framework helps identify the impact of these actions (Impact) and offers actionable suggestions for improvement (Next Steps). Additionally, encouraging the recipient to reflect on the feedback (Reflection) and fostering a deeper understanding of their own actions and their effects on others (Self-Awareness) ensure that feedback leads to meaningful growth. This approach not only addresses immediate issues but also builds a foundation for continuous development and stronger, more effective leadership.

THE PURPOSE OF FEEDBACK

At its core, feedback is a vital communication tool that provides individuals with valuable insights into their actions, behaviors, and attitudes. It serves as a mirror, reflecting one's performance against established expectations and standards. Whether in the workplace, classroom or within interpersonal relationships, feedback acts as a compass, guiding individuals towards alignment with their goals and aspirations.

Feedback serves a dual purpose: it informs and inspires. By offering constructive criticism or praise, feedback provides individuals with the necessary information to assess their performance and make informed decisions for improvement. Moreover, feedback serves as a catalyst for growth, igniting motivation and inspiring individuals to strive for excellence.

Feedback bridges the gap between current performance and desired outcomes, paving the way for continuous learning and development. It empowers individuals to recognize their strengths, acknowledge areas for improvement, and take proactive steps toward personal and professional advancement.

WHY FEEDBACK MATTERS

The significance of feedback cannot be overstated. It is the lifeblood of learning and development, fueling progress and innovation across various domains. Feedback fosters a culture of continuous improvement by allowing individuals to reflect on their actions, receive guidance, and refine their skills.

Effective feedback enhances performance by clearly understanding individuals' strengths and weaknesses. It acts as a catalyst for self-awareness, enabling individuals to identify blind spots and areas for growth. Moreover, feedback strengthens relationships by fostering open communication, trust, and mutual respect. When delivered with empathy and sincerity, feedback builds bridges, deepens connections, and cultivates a supportive environment conducive to growth and collaboration.

Conversely, the absence of feedback can lead to complacency, disengagement, and stagnation. Without constructive input, individuals may struggle to identify areas for improvement or recognize the impact of their actions on others. As a result, growth opportunities may be overlooked, and potential may remain untapped.

CHAPTER 1

FOUNDATIONS OF EFFECTIVE FEEDBACK

In this book, we will embark on a journey to explore the multifaceted nature of feedback, uncovering its psychological foundations, diverse forms, effective techniques, and real-world applications. Each chapter is meticulously crafted to provide readers with a comprehensive understanding of feedback and its transformative power. As we navigate through the complexities of feedback, we introduce the *concept of constructive insights*, which go beyond traditional feedback by providing a deeper understanding and context to foster continuous improvement and innovation. Constructive insights offer a more relatable approach to feedback and highlight its potential to drive personal and professional growth in a rapidly evolving world.

In Chapter 2, we will examine the psychological underpinnings of feedback, delving into its cognitive and emotional dimensions. We explore how feedback influences behaviors, motivations, and self-perceptions through theories such as Cognitive Dissonance, Self-Regulation, Social Cognitive Theory, and Neuroplasticity. We also discuss the emotional impact of feedback and how it can elicit a range of responses. By understanding these mechanisms, readers will understand how feedback can be used more effectively. Constructive insights are emphasized as a powerful tool for aligning cognitive and emotional responses, promoting resilience, and enhancing self-efficacy.

Next, in Chapters 3 and 4, we will explore the various types of feedback, from praise to constructive criticism and examine their respective roles in driving growth and development. We discuss the benefits and drawbacks of each type and introduce constructive insights as a superior approach that combines elements of both praise and criticism. This chapter emphasizes how constructive insights can provide a balanced perspective, encouraging acknowledgment of strengths and identifying areas for improvement.

Chapter 5 delves into the art and science of giving feedback, offering practical strategies and frameworks for effective communication. We cover essential techniques such as the SBI (Situation-Behavior-Impact) model, the DESC (Describe-Express-Specify-Consequences) script, and the use of constructive insights to provide nuanced and context-rich feedback. Readers will learn how to deliver clear, specific, and actionable feedback, fostering an environment of trust and continuous improvement.

Receiving feedback can be challenging but crucial for growth and development. This chapter offers strategies for receiving feedback with an open mind and a growth mindset. We discuss how to constructively process and act on feedback, using it as a tool for self-reflection and personal growth. Constructive insights play a key role here, as they help individuals understand the broader context of the feedback and how to apply it effectively.

Feedback is often surrounded by challenges and misconceptions that can hinder its effectiveness. This chapter addresses common obstacles such as fear of criticism, defensiveness, and misinterpreting feedback. We provide readers with tools to overcome these barriers and embrace feedback as a catalyst for change. By incorporating constructive insights, we show how feedback can be reframed to emphasize learning and development rather than judgment.

In Chapters 6-8, we will examine the role of feedback in various contexts, from the classroom to the boardroom, shedding light on its impact on education, workplace dynamics, and personal relationships. We illustrate how feedback practices can be adapted to different environments through insightful case studies and real-world examples. Constructive insights are highlighted as a versatile approach that can be tailored to meet the unique needs of each context, enhancing effectiveness and fostering positive outcomes.

This chapter presents case studies and real-world examples of how feedback culture has been implemented and its impact on various organizations, educational institutions, and individuals. We uncover the transformative power of feedback in driving innovation, fostering growth, and enhancing performance. By showcasing the successful application of constructive insights, we demonstrate their potential to profoundly shape lives and organizations.

As we will look to the future, we explore constructive insights as the next evolution in feedback. We discuss how this approach integrates the best aspects of traditional feedback while providing deeper, more meaningful guidance. Constructive insights are positioned as a key strategy for addressing the complexities of a multi-generational workforce, fostering inclusivity, and promoting continuous learning and innovation.

In the final chapters (9-12), we summarize the key takeaways from the book and provide a call to action for readers to embrace the principles of effective feedback and constructive insights. We encourage readers to apply the strategies and frameworks discussed in their personal and professional lives, embarking on a journey of self-discovery, empowerment, and transformation.

In essence, this book serves as a roadmap for harnessing the power of feedback to unlock potential, drive growth, and foster meaningful connections. By understanding the intricacies of feedback and embracing the concept of constructive insights, readers will embark on a journey of self-discovery, empowerment, and transformation. Through this comprehensive exploration, we aim to equip individuals and organizations with the knowledge and tools to create a culture of continuous improvement and success.

CHAPTER 2:

THE PSYCHOLOGICAL BASIS OF FEEDBACK

Feedback is not merely a transactional exchange of information; it operates on a profound psychological level, shaping behaviors, motivations, and self-perceptions. This chapter delves into the intricate mechanisms through which feedback influences cognition, emotion, and behavior, shedding light on its transformative power.

THE SCIENCE BEHIND FEEDBACK

1. The Cognitive Mechanisms of Feedback

Cognitive Dissonance Theory: Feedback can trigger cognitive dissonance, a psychological state where individuals experience discomfort due to a discrepancy between their beliefs and actions. Festinger's (1957) Cognitive Dissonance Theory explains how feedback can drive behavioral change by highlighting inconsistencies between self-perception and external evaluation. For example, when an employee believes they are performing well but receives feedback indicating areas for improvement, the resulting dissonance can motivate them to adjust their behavior to align with the feedback.

Self-Regulation and Goal Setting: Feedback plays a crucial role in self-regulation, helping individuals monitor their progress toward goals. According to Carver and Scheier's (1998) Control Theory, feedback is a comparator that individuals use to assess the difference between their current state and desired goals. Positive feedback reinforces goal-directed behaviors, while negative feedback signals the need for corrective action. Research by Locke and Latham (2002) further supports this, demonstrating that specific and challenging goals, coupled with appropriate feedback, significantly enhance performance.

Social Cognitive Theory: Bandura's (1986) Social Cognitive Theory emphasizes the role of feedback in learning and behavior modification. Feedback provides external reinforcement, shaping self-efficacy and outcome expectations. When individuals receive constructive feedback, their belief in their ability to succeed (self-efficacy) is strengthened, leading to increased motivation and persistence. A meta-analysis by Sitzmann and Yeo (2013) confirms that self-efficacy strongly predicts performance, particularly when individuals receive consistent and constructive feedback.

Cognitive Load Theory: Feedback can influence cognitive load, which refers to the amount of mental effort required to process information. Sweller's (1988) Cognitive Load Theory suggests that feedback can help manage intrinsic and extraneous cognitive load by providing clear, concise information that facilitates learning. Effective feedback reduces cognitive overload, allowing individuals to focus on essential learning tasks and improve their performance.

2. The Emotional Impact of Feedback

Emotional Reactions: Feedback can elicit various emotions, from joy and pride to anxiety and frustration. Kluger and DeNisi's (1996) Feedback Intervention Theory (FIT) suggests that feedback affects individuals' emotional states by focusing their attention on specific aspects of their performance. Positive feedback tends to enhance self-esteem and motivation, while negative feedback can cause emotional distress and promote self-improvement when delivered constructively. A study by Ilies and Judge (2005) found that feedback significantly influences job satisfaction and emotional well-being, with positive feedback enhancing these outcomes.

Affective Events Theory: Weiss and Cropanzano's (1996) Affective Events Theory (AET) posits that workplace events, including feedback, generate emotional reactions that influence work attitudes and behaviors. Positive feedback can lead to positive emotions, enhancing job satisfaction and performance. Conversely, negative feedback can trigger negative emotions, potentially reducing job satisfaction and motivating corrective actions. AET highlights the importance of managing the emotional impact of feedback to maintain a positive and productive work environment.

Mood and Performance: Research by Staw, Sutton, and Pelled (1994) indicates that positive moods induced by positive feedback can lead to higher levels of creativity, problem-solving, and overall job performance. Conversely, negative feedback can lead to defensive reactions and reduced performance if not managed properly. Therefore, how feedback is delivered can significantly influence the emotional and behavioral outcomes.

3. Behavioral Outcomes of Feedback

Behavioral Change: Feedback has a direct impact on behavior modification. Thorndike's (1911) Law of Effect states that behaviors followed by positive consequences are likely to be repeated, while those followed by negative consequences are less likely to recur. Effective feedback reinforces desired behaviors and discourages undesired ones, shaping overall performance. A study by Podsakoff and Farh (1989) showed that positive feedback significantly enhances task performance and organizational citizenship behaviors.

Feedback-Seeking Behavior: Research by Ashford and Cummings (1983) highlights the proactive aspect of feedback, where individuals actively seek feedback to improve their performance and self-perception. Feedback-seeking behavior is driven by a desire for self-improvement and accuracy in self-assessment. This behavior is influenced by factors such as self-esteem, the perceived utility of feedback, and the organizational culture. Studies have shown that feedback-seeking behavior improves job performance, career progression, and professional development (Anseel, Beatty, Shen, Lievens, & Sackett, 2015).

Behavioral Insights and Nudge Theory: Thaler and Sunstein's (2008) Nudge Theory suggests that feedback can serve as a nudge to influence behavior in subtle but powerful ways. For example, providing feedback on energy consumption can lead individuals to adopt more energy-efficient behaviors. In organizational settings, feedback can nudge employees towards adopting healthier habits, improving productivity, and enhancing overall well-being.

4. The Transformative Power of Feedback

Growth Mindset: Carol Dweck's (2006) research on fixed versus growth mindsets illustrates the transformative potential of feedback. Individuals with growth mindset view feedback as an opportunity to learn and grow, while those with a fixed mindset may see it as a judgment of their abilities. Encouraging a growth mindset through constructive feedback can foster resilience, adaptability, and continuous improvement. Research by Yeager and Dweck (2012) found that students with a growth mindset performed better academically and were more resilient in facing challenges.

Neuroplasticity: Recent studies in neuroscience, such as those by Draganski et al. (2004), demonstrate that feedback can facilitate neuroplasticity—the brain's ability to reorganize itself by forming new neural connections. Constructive feedback can lead to cognitive and behavioral changes by reinforcing new learning pathways, ultimately transforming an individual's skill set and capabilities. This is particularly evident in skill acquisition and habit formation, where consistent feedback leads to lasting changes in neural pathways.

Self-Determination Theory: Deci and Ryan's (2000) Self-Determination Theory emphasize the role of feedback in fulfilling the basic psychological needs of autonomy, competence, and relatedness. Constructive feedback enhances individuals' sense of competence and autonomy, leading to higher intrinsic motivation and better performance. Research supports that feedback fulfilling these needs increases job satisfaction, commitment, and overall well-being (Gagné & Deci, 2005).

5. Practical Applications

Feedback in Education: Hattie and Timperley's (2007) meta-analysis on feedback in educational settings underscores its significant impact on student achievement. Effective feedback provides clear, specific, and timely information that helps students understand their learning progress and areas needing improvement. Black and Wiliam (1998) found that formative assessment and feedback significantly improve student learning outcomes. Constructive feedback focused on the learning process rather than the person can foster a growth mindset and encourage persistence.

Feedback in the Workplace: A Gallup (2019) study found that employees who receive regular feedback are 3.6 times more likely to be engaged at work. Regular, constructive feedback fosters a sense of purpose and direction, enhancing overall performance and job satisfaction. Another study by Zenger and Folkman (2014) found that employees prefer corrective feedback to praise if it is delivered constructively and helps them improve.

Feedback in Therapy: Feedback is critical to cognitive-behavioral therapy (CBT) in therapeutic settings. Research by Lambert et al. (2003) indicates that client outcomes improve significantly when therapists incorporate regular feedback on client progress, facilitating adjustments to treatment plans and promoting self-awareness. A Lambert and Shimokawa (2011) meta-analysis confirmed that feedback-informed therapy significantly enhances treatment effectiveness and client satisfaction.

Feedback is a powerful psychological tool influencing cognition, emotion, and behavior. By understanding the underlying mechanisms, such as cognitive dissonance, self-regulation, emotional reactions, neuroplasticity, and self-determination, we can harness the transformative power of feedback to drive personal and professional growth. Whether in educational settings, workplaces, or therapy, effective feedback fosters self-improvement, enhances performance, and ultimately leads to the realization of individual potential. Through strategically implementing feedback practices, individuals and organizations can create environments that promote continuous learning, resilience, and success.

HOW FEEDBACK INFLUENCES BEHAVIOR

Feedback catalyzes behavior change by tapping into the fundamental human drive to minimize discrepancies between one's current state and desired goals. When individuals receive feedback, they engage in a process of comparison, evaluating their performance against established standards or expectations. Positive feedback reinforces desired behaviors, signaling to individuals that they are on the right track. Conversely, constructive criticism highlights areas needing improvement, providing individuals with actionable insights on enhancing their performance.

The effectiveness of feedback in shaping behavior lies in its ability to provide specific, actionable information. By clarifying what needs to be maintained or changed, feedback empowers individuals to make informed decisions and take proactive steps toward achieving their objectives. It serves as a roadmap for improvement, guiding individuals towards better performance and outcomes.

COACHING CORNER

Workplace Performance Review: In a corporate setting, feedback shapes employee behavior and performance. Employees receive constructive criticism from their manager during a quarterly performance review regarding their presentation skills. The feedback highlights specific areas for improvement such as maintaining eye contact, using more engaging visuals, and speaking clearly. This actionable feedback provides the employee with clear guidance on enhancing their presentation skills. As a result, the employee actively implements the suggested changes, leading to noticeable improvements in subsequent presentations. The feedback serves as a catalyst for behavior change, aligning the employee's actions with the desired performance standards.

Sales Performance Evaluation: During a quarterly sales performance review, a sales representative receives feedback from their supervisor regarding their sales techniques. The supervisor highlights that while the representative has successfully met sales targets, there's room for improvement in building long-term client relationships. The feedback includes specific suggestions such as personalized follow-up emails and regular check-ins to understand client needs better. Armed with this feedback, the sales representative adjusts their approach, focusing on nurturing client connections rather than solely pursuing new leads. Over the following months, the representative sees an increase in repeat business and positive client feedback, indicating a successful behavior change influenced by the feedback received.

Project Management Assessment: In a project management review meeting, a project manager receives feedback from stakeholders regarding their leadership style and project execution. While the project was completed within the deadline, stakeholders expressed concerns about communication breakdowns and delays in decision-making. The feedback prompts the project manager to reassess their communication strategy and decision-making processes. Implementing the feedback, the project manager adopts a more transparent communication approach, holding regular meetings to update stakeholders and streamline decision-making protocols. As a result, subsequent projects see improved coordination, reduced delays, and higher stakeholder satisfaction, showcasing the tangible impact of feedback on behavior and performance.

Team Collaboration Evaluation: During a team performance review, team members provide feedback to each other on their collaboration and teamwork skills. One team member receives feedback that they tend to dominate discussions during meetings, which hinders other team members from contributing their ideas effectively. This feedback prompts the individual to reflect on their communication style and actively seek input from others. In subsequent meetings, the team member consciously encourages participation from all team members, listens attentively to their ideas, and facilitates inclusive discussions. The shift in behavior leads to improved team dynamics, increased engagement from all members, and ultimately, enhanced productivity and innovation within the team.

Fitness Training Session: In a fitness training session, a personal trainer provides feedback to a client on their exercise technique. During a strength training exercise, the trainer observes that the client's form is slightly off, potentially risking injury. The trainer offers constructive criticism, explaining the proper form and providing hands-on guidance to correct the client's posture. By addressing the issue promptly and offering specific feedback, the trainer empowers the client to make immediate adjustments, ensuring safer and more effective workouts. The feedback influences the client's behavior by instilling a greater focus on maintaining correct form during future exercises, ultimately contributing to their long-term fitness goals.

Academic Tutoring Session: In an academic tutoring session, a student receives feedback on their essay writing skills. The tutor reviews the student's essay and identifies areas where the argument lacks clarity and coherence. Through constructive criticism, the tutor offers suggestions for restructuring the essay and providing additional supporting evidence. The feedback provides the student with actionable insights on how to improve their writing technique. With a clearer understanding of what aspects of their writing need refinement, the student revises the essay accordingly, integrating the feedback to enhance its overall quality. The feedback loop in this tutoring session influences the student's behavior by encouraging them to apply the suggested improvements in future writing assignments, ultimately fostering academic growth and success.

THE ROLE OF FEEDBACK IN MOTIVATION AND SELF-ESTEEM

Feedback plays a pivotal role in motivation, serving as both a source of encouragement and a catalyst for change. Positive feedback has the power to boost confidence and reinforce individuals' belief in their abilities. It provides validation and recognition for their efforts, fueling a sense of accomplishment and satisfaction. Moreover, positive feedback serves as a motivator, encouraging individuals to continue their pursuit of excellence and strive for even greater success.

On the other hand, constructive feedback, when delivered appropriately, can serve as a powerful motivator for improvement. By highlighting areas in need of development, constructive criticism challenges individuals to push beyond their comfort zones and reach new heights. It fosters a growth mindset, instilling a belief in the possibility of improvement and the value of continuous learning.

Furthermore, feedback influences individuals' self-esteem, shaping their perceptions of themselves and their capabilities. Consistent, balanced feedback helps individuals develop a realistic and positive self-image. Positive feedback reaffirms individuals' strengths and accomplishments, reinforcing their sense of self-worth. Similarly, constructive criticism, when delivered with empathy and respect, helps individuals recognize areas for growth without undermining their self-esteem.

COACHING CORNER

"The Feedback Loop"

In the bustling city of Málaga in Spain, nestled amidst towering skyscrapers and bustling streets, there stood a quaint café named "Perk & Brew." It was a place where locals sought refuge from the chaos of urban life, indulging in steaming cups of coffee and engaging conversations.

At the heart of Perk & Brew was Sarah, a barista with a passion for crafting the perfect cup of coffee. Her dedication to her craft was unparalleled, but she harbored a secret ambition – to become a master barista renowned for her signature blends.

One day, as Sarah meticulously prepared a latte art masterpiece for a regular customer, she overheard murmurs of excitement from a group of coffee aficionados sitting at a nearby table. They were discussing an upcoming barista competition, where the winner would earn recognition and a coveted spot at an elite coffee expo.

Intrigued by the prospect of showcasing her skills on a larger stage, Sarah decided to enter the competition. With determination fueling her every move, she spent countless hours perfecting her techniques, experimenting with new flavor profiles, and seeking feedback from her customers.

As the competition day approached, nerves tingled through Sarah's veins. Standing behind the espresso machine in the competition arena, she felt a mix of excitement and apprehension. The judges, renowned coffee connoisseurs themselves, scrutinized each contestant's creations with keen eyes.

With steady hands, Sarah poured her heart and soul into crafting her signature blend – a delicate balance of Ethiopian beans with hints of dark chocolate and floral undertones. As she presented her creation to the judges, she held her breath, awaiting their verdict.

The room fell silent as the judges sipped Sarah's creation; their expressions inscrutable. Finally, one of them spoke, his voice carrying across the room with authority. "Remarkable," he declared, a hint of awe in his tone. "This blend possesses a complexity of flavors that is truly exceptional."

Sarah's heart soared with joy as the judges praised her craftsmanship. But it wasn't just the victory that filled her with pride – it was the journey of growth and self-discovery that led her to this moment. She realized that feedback from customers, peers, or experts had been the guiding force behind her success.

In the following weeks, Sarah's reputation as a master barista spread far and wide. Customers flocked to Perk & Brew, eager to taste her award-winning creations. As Sarah continued to hone her skills, she remained ever grateful for the feedback that had shaped her journey—a testament to the power of the feedback loop in fueling personal and professional growth.

COGNITIVE AND EMOTIONAL RESPONSES TO FEEDBACK

Receiving feedback triggers a range of cognitive and emotional responses, shaping individuals' reactions and subsequent behavior. Initially, feedback may evoke cognitive dissonance—discomfort resulting from perceived discrepancies between self-image and feedback received. Individuals may experience defensiveness or resistance to feedback that challenges their beliefs or behaviors.

However, with a shift in perspective, feedback can serve as a catalyst for introspection and growth. Constructive criticism, when processed positively, prompts individuals to reflect on their actions and consider alternative approaches. It fosters self-awareness, enabling individuals to recognize their strengths and weaknesses more accurately.

Moreover, feedback influences individuals' emotional responses, shaping their overall experience and receptiveness to feedback. Positive feedback elicits feelings of pride, validation, and satisfaction, reinforcing individuals' motivation and engagement. Conversely, constructive criticism may initially evoke feelings of discomfort or vulnerability. However, when delivered with empathy and support, constructive feedback can inspire individuals to embrace challenges and pursue self-improvement.

Understanding these cognitive and emotional responses to feedback is essential for designing feedback interventions that are not only informative but also supportive and encouraging. By acknowledging and addressing individuals' reactions to feedback, we can create an environment conducive to growth and development, where feedback serves as a catalyst for positive change.

COACHING CORNER

Neurological Responses to Feedback Processing. Neuroimaging studies have provided insights into the cognitive and emotional responses triggered by feedback. Research using techniques such as functional magnetic resonance imaging (fMRI) has shown that receiving feedback activates areas of the brain associated with self-awareness, such as the anterior cingulate cortex (ACC) and medial prefrontal cortex (mPFC).

These regions are implicated in processing information related to self-relevance and social evaluation, indicating that feedback processing involves a cognitive appraisal of one's self-image in relation to external feedback. Additionally, studies have demonstrated that feedback, particularly when perceived as negative or discrepant from one's self-concept, can elicit emotional responses mediated by the amygdala, a brain region involved in processing emotions such as fear and anxiety. This neurological evidence suggests that feedback processing is a complex interplay between cognitive evaluation and emotional reactivity, with implications for understanding how individuals interpret and respond to feedback in various contexts.

Psychophysiological Responses to Feedback Receptivity: Psychophysiological research has investigated how individuals' physiological responses correlate with their receptivity to feedback. Studies utilizing heart rate variability (HRV) measures and galvanic skin response (GSR) have found that feedback-induced arousal levels influence individuals' cognitive processing and emotional reactions. For example, when individuals receive positive feedback, HRV patterns indicative of increased parasympathetic nervous system activity suggest a state of relaxation and receptiveness.

In contrast, receiving negative or critical feedback may trigger sympathetic nervous system activation, reflected in heightened GSR levels associated with stress and defensive responses. These psychophysiological markers objectively measure individuals' cognitive and emotional engagement with feedback, shedding light on the underlying mechanisms driving feedback processing and behavioral adaptation.

Behavioral Responses to Feedback Modulation: Behavioral studies have explored how individuals' cognitive and emotional responses to feedback influence subsequent behavior and decision-making. Experimental paradigms involving feedback manipulation have shown that framing feedback in a supportive and constructive manner enhances individuals' receptivity and willingness to engage in reflective processing.

For instance, providing feedback in a non-threatening context or coupling constructive criticism with positive reinforcement can mitigate defensive reactions and promote constructive responses. Moreover, longitudinal research has demonstrated that interventions that foster a growth mindset – the belief that abilities can be developed through effort and learning – can modulate individuals' cognitive appraisals of feedback, leading to greater resilience and adaptive behavior in the face of challenges. These findings underscore the importance of considering cognitive and emotional factors in designing effective feedback interventions that facilitate learning and personal development.

CHAPTER 3:

TYPES OF FEEDBACK

Feedback comes in various forms, each serving a distinct purpose and context. In this chapter, we explore the different types of feedback, from praise to constructive criticism, and examine their respective roles in driving growth and development.

POSITIVE FEEDBACK

Positive feedback serves as a powerful tool for reinforcing desired behaviors and accomplishments. It shines a spotlight on individuals' strengths and achievements, validating and recognizing their efforts. By highlighting what individuals are doing well, positive feedback boosts morale and motivation, inspiring them to continue their pursuit of excellence. Moreover, positive feedback fosters a positive organizational culture where appreciation and recognition are valued, increasing engagement and job satisfaction.

In addition to its motivational benefits, positive feedback encourages the repetition of desired actions, reinforcing individuals' confidence in their abilities. It serves as a catalyst for building self-esteem, instilling a sense of pride and accomplishment in individuals' achievements. Incorporating positive feedback into our interactions creates an environment where individuals feel valued and supported, laying the foundation for sustained success and growth.

COACHING CORNER

The following feedback highlights specific achievements, offers genuine praise, and emphasizes the positive impact of the individual's contributions, thereby boosting morale and encouraging continued excellence.

I was thoroughly impressed with your creativity and meticulous attention to detail during the recent team presentation. Your innovative approach in designing the slides and the clear, compelling narrative you crafted truly stood out. Your ability to convey complex information in an accessible and engaging manner is a testament to your exceptional communication skills.

Your dedication and hard work were evident, and the positive feedback we received from the clients underscores the effectiveness of your efforts. By consistently delivering such high-quality work, you contribute significantly to our team's success and set a high standard for excellence.

Keep up the fantastic work! Your contributions are highly valued, and your commitment to excellence inspires everyone around you. It's clear that you are a key asset to our team, and I look forward to seeing your continued growth and success. `

CONSTRUCTIVE INSIGHTS

Constructive insights plays a crucial role in fostering growth and development. Unlike praise, which focuses on individuals' strengths, constructive insights highlights areas for improvement and offers suggestions for change. It provides individuals with valuable insights into their performance, guiding them towards enhanced skills and competencies.

One of the key features of constructive insights is its focus on specific behaviors or actions rather than personal attributes. By addressing behaviors rather than individuals' inherent qualities, constructive insights reduces defensiveness and encourages receptiveness to feedback. Moreover, constructive insights provides individuals with a roadmap for improvement, outlining actionable steps to enhance their performance.

When delivered effectively, constructive insights fosters a culture of continuous improvement, where feedback is viewed as an opportunity for growth rather than a critique of one's abilities. It encourages individuals to embrace challenges and seek out opportunities for self-improvement. By incorporating constructive insights into our feedback practices, we create an environment where feedback is valued and individuals are empowered to reach their full potential.

COACHING CORNER

The Tale of the Valiant Innovator

Gather around, dear colleagues, for I have a tale to share—a tale of triumph, perseverance, and the extraordinary feats of one of our own. Allow me to regale you with the story of Robert, whose recent exploits have woven into our team's lore.

In the heart of our bustling organization, amidst the hum of productivity and the buzz of innovation, there dwelled a visionary named Robert. With a twinkle in his eye and a fire in his heart, he embarked on a quest to revolutionize our approach to documentation management .

The journey began with a spark of inspiration—a bold idea that promised to reshape the landscape of our industry. Undeterred by the challenges that lay ahead, Robert set forth with determination, armed with ingenuity and an unwavering belief in his vision.

As they traversed the treacherous terrain of uncertainty and doubt, Robert faced formidable adversaries—technical hurdles, logistical obstacles, and the ever-looming specter of failure. Yet, with each setback encountered, he emerged stronger and more resolute, refusing to yield to the forces that sought to impede his progress.

Through sheer grit and boundless creativity, Robert blazed a trail of innovation, devising ingenious solutions to seemingly insurmountable problems. His perseverance inspired awe among his peers, breathing new life into our team's collective spirit and propelling us closer to our shared goals.

And then, amidst the swirling maelstrom of challenges, came the moment of reckoning—a triumphant breakthrough that sent ripples of excitement throughout our organization. Robert's groundbreaking innovation had come to fruition, unleashing a wave of transformative change reverberating far and wide.

Standing on the precipice of a new era, let us raise our voices to celebrate Robert's remarkable achievements. His courage, creativity, and unwavering determination have not only reshaped our team's trajectory but have also left an indelible mark on the annals of our organization's history.

So, here's to Robert, the valiant innovator whose bold vision has illuminated our path forward. May his story serve as a testament to the power of perseverance, the magic of innovation, and the boundless potential within each of us.

FORMAL VS. INFORMAL FEEDBACK

Feedback can be classified into two broad categories: formal and informal. Formal feedback is structured and often part of a process, where individuals receive feedback on their performance against predetermined goals and objectives. It is typically documented and may involve a formal meeting between the individual and their supervisor or manager.

On the other hand, informal feedback occurs spontaneously and is part of day-to-day interactions between colleagues, peers, or mentors. It may be casual conversations, impromptu meetings, or quick check-ins. Informal feedback is often more immediate and personalized, providing individuals with timely insights into their performance and behavior.

Both formal and informal feedback are valuable and serve different purposes and contexts. Formal feedback provides individuals with a comprehensive performance assessment, highlighting strengths, areas for improvement, and developmental opportunities. It facilitates goal setting, performance management, and career development. In contrast, informal feedback offers individuals more immediate, real-time insights into their performance, enabling them to make timely adjustments and improvements. It fosters open communication and collaboration, strengthening relationships and promoting continuous learning and improvement.

COACHING CORNER

Formal Feedback:

Formal feedback at XYZ Corporation is a structured process designed to provide employees with a comprehensive assessment of their performance in alignment with predetermined goals and objectives. Let's consider the example of Sarah, a marketing executive at XYZ Corporation, who recently underwent a formal feedback session with her manager, John.

Sarah's formal feedback session began with a meeting in John's office, where they discussed Sarah's performance over the past quarter. John had prepared detailed documentation outlining Sarah's achievements, areas of improvement, and developmental opportunities based on her performance against key performance indicators (KPIs) and established goals.

During the meeting, John reviewed Sarah's accomplishments, commending her for exceeding customer acquisition and retention targets. He also acknowledged Sarah's successful execution of the latest marketing campaign, which significantly increased brand visibility and engagement.

However, John also provided constructive criticism regarding Sarah's time management skills, noting instances where deadlines were missed, or projects were delayed. He emphasized the importance of prioritization and offered guidance on how Sarah could improve her organizational skills to better meet project timelines in the future.

Throughout the formal feedback session, John maintained a professional demeanor, ensuring the feedback was objective, specific, and actionable. He encouraged Sarah to reflect on her performance and actively participate in setting new goals and action plans for the upcoming quarter.

Sarah's formal feedback session with John gave her a comprehensive assessment of her performance, highlighting her accomplishments and areas for improvement. It was a valuable tool for performance management and career development, setting clear expectations and goals for Sarah's continued growth and success at XYZ Corporation.

Informal Feedback:

In contrast to formal feedback, informal feedback at XYZ Corporation occurs spontaneously as part of day-to-day interactions between colleagues, peers, or mentors. Let's explore how Sarah, the marketing executive, receives informal feedback from her colleagues during a team meeting.

During a weekly team meeting, Sarah updates her colleagues on her latest marketing campaign. After her presentation, Sarah's colleague, Alex, approached her and offered informal feedback.

"Hey Sarah, great job on the campaign presentation! I loved how you incorporated the latest market trends into your strategy. It really resonated with our target audience," Alex says with a smile.

Sarah appreciates Alex's positive feedback and takes note of his comments. However, Alex also offers suggestions for improvement. "One thing I noticed is that the call-to-action in your email copy could be more compelling. Maybe we could A/B test different versions to see which one performs better," Alex suggests.

Sarah listens attentively to Alex's feedback and expresses gratitude for his insights. She jots down Alex's suggestion and makes a mental note to revisit the email copy for optimization.

Throughout the team meeting, Sarah receives additional informal feedback from her colleagues, ranging from praise for her creativity to suggestions for refining her marketing strategies. Each interaction gives Sarah valuable insights into her performance, enabling her to make timely adjustments and improvements.

Informal feedback at XYZ Corporation offers Sarah more immediate, real-time insights into her performance, fostering open communication and collaboration among team members. It complements the formal feedback process by providing Sarah with personalized feedback that enhances her professional development and contributes to the team's overall success.

REAL-TIME VS. DELAYED FEEDBACK

Feedback can also be categorized based on its timing: real-time or delayed. Real-time feedback is immediate and can address issues as they arise, providing individuals with timely insights into their performance and behavior. It is often delivered in the moment, allowing individuals to make immediate adjustments and improvements. Real-time feedback is particularly effective in correcting behaviors quickly and reinforcing desired actions.

In contrast, delayed feedback is given after some time has passed, allowing individuals to reflect and analyze. It may occur as part of a formal performance review process or during scheduled feedback sessions. Delayed feedback gives individuals a more comprehensive assessment of their performance, allowing for a deeper understanding of their strengths, areas for improvement, and developmental needs.

Each form of feedback has its advantages and serves different purposes and contexts. Real-time feedback addresses issues promptly and reinforces desired behaviors, while delayed feedback provides individuals with a more holistic view of their performance and behavior. By incorporating real-time and delayed feedback into our feedback practices, we create a balanced approach promoting continuous learning and improvement.

COACHING CORNER

Real-Time Feedback:

At Acme Innovations, real-time feedback is an integral part of our culture, empowering employees to address issues and maximize performance in the moment. Let's explore how real-time feedback plays out in a scenario involving Debra, a software engineer working on a critical project.

As Debra diligently works on coding a new feature for a software release, her colleague, Scott, notices a potential bug in her code. Rather than waiting for the end of the day or a scheduled meeting, Scott approaches Debra immediately to provide real-time feedback.

"Hey Debra, I just reviewed your code for the new feature, and I noticed a potential bug in the validation function. It seems like the input validation logic might not catch certain edge cases. I thought you might want to take a look before proceeding further," Scott says, offering his insights with a supportive tone.

Debra appreciates Scott's real-time feedback and immediately reviews the code snippet in question. She identifies the issue and makes the necessary corrections, ensuring the code meets the project's quality standards.

Thanks to Scott's timely intervention, Debra can address the bug before it escalates, saving valuable time and resources for the team. The real-time feedback helps Debra improve her coding skills and reinforces a culture of collaboration and continuous improvement within the team.

Delayed Feedback:

While real-time feedback addresses issues as they arise, delayed feedback gives individuals a more comprehensive assessment of their performance over time. Let's explore how delayed feedback unfolds in a scenario involving Debra's participation in a quarterly performance review.

As the end of the quarter approaches, Debra sits down with her manager, Scott, for a scheduled performance review. During the meeting, Scott provides Debra with delayed feedback based on her performance throughout the quarter.

"Debra, I want to commend you for your outstanding contributions to the team this quarter. Your attention to detail and commitment to delivering high-quality work has not gone unnoticed," Scott begins, offering genuine praise for Debra's efforts.

However, Scott also takes the opportunity to address areas where Debra can further improve. He provides specific examples of instances where Debra's communication could have been clearer or her project management skills more refined.

"As we look ahead to the next quarter, I encourage you to focus on refining your communication skills and prioritizing tasks more effectively. With a few adjustments, I do not doubt that you'll continue to excel in your role," Scott concludes, offering constructive feedback aimed at Debra's professional growth.

Debra appreciates Scott's thoughtful feedback and takes notes to reflect on his insights. The delayed feedback gives Debra a more holistic view of her performance, allowing her to identify patterns and areas for development over time.

Both real-time and delayed feedback are important in promoting continuous learning and improvement at Acme Innovations. Real-time feedback enables quick course corrections and reinforces desired behaviors, while delayed feedback offers a deeper understanding of performance trends and opportunities for growth. By incorporating both forms of feedback into our feedback practices, we create a balanced approach that empowers employees to thrive and succeed in their roles.

CHAPTER 4:

FEEDBACK IN DIFFERENT CONTEXTS

Feedback is a universal tool that transcends boundaries and finds application in various spheres of life. In this chapter, we explore how feedback manifests in different contexts—education, the workplace, personal relationships, and customer service—and examine its role in driving growth, fostering communication, and enhancing performance.

FEEDBACK IN EDUCATION

In educational settings, feedback serves as a cornerstone of student development. It plays a pivotal role in guiding students' learning process, helping them understand their strengths and weaknesses, and identifying areas for improvement. Effective feedback provides students with actionable insights into their performance, enabling them to refine their skills and achieve academic success.

Moreover, feedback in education promotes a growth mindset, instilling in students the belief that their abilities can be developed through effort and perseverance. By acknowledging students' efforts and providing constructive guidance, educators empower students to take ownership of their learning journey and strive for continuous improvement.

Furthermore, feedback in education is not limited to formal assessments or grading systems; it encompasses a wide range of interactions, including classroom discussions, peer evaluations, and teacher-student conferences. These varied feedback forms create a supportive learning environment where students feel valued, motivated, and empowered to reach their full potential.

FEEDBACK IN THE WORKPLACE

In the workplace, feedback is a driving force behind performance and development. It serves as a linchpin in the employee-employer relationship, facilitating communication, setting expectations, and fostering a culture of continuous improvement. Effective feedback helps employees understand their role within the organization, align their efforts with organizational goals, and identify opportunities for growth and development.

Feedback in the workplace occurs through various channels, including formal performance reviews, one-on-one meetings, and peer evaluations. These interactions give employees valuable insights into their performance, enabling them to course-correct, refine their skills, and enhance their organizational contributions.

Moreover, feedback in the workplace promotes accountability and transparency, ensuring that expectations are clearly communicated and understood by all parties involved. By fostering open communication and collaboration, feedback cultivates a culture of trust, respect, and mutual support, where employees feel valued, empowered, and motivated to excel.

FEEDBACK IN PERSONAL RELATIONSHIPS

Feedback is a cornerstone of communication and understanding in personal relationships. It helps individuals navigate interpersonal dynamics, resolve conflicts, and build stronger, more supportive connections. Effective feedback involves expressing thoughts, feelings, and concerns in a constructive and empathetic manner, with the aim of fostering mutual growth and harmony.

Feedback in personal relationships encompasses various interactions, from casual conversations to more formal discussions. Whether offering praise, expressing gratitude, or addressing areas for improvement, feedback creates a safe space for individuals to share their thoughts and feelings openly and honestly.

Moreover, feedback in personal relationships promotes empathy and understanding, enabling individuals to see things from each other's perspectives and work towards common goals. By fostering open communication, active listening, and respect for each other's feelings, feedback strengthens bonds, builds trust, and nurtures meaningful connections that withstand the test of time.

FEEDBACK IN CUSTOMER SERVICE

Feedback is a critical component of business improvement in customer service. It provides insights into customer satisfaction, preferences, and pain points, enabling organizations to deliver products and services that meet or exceed customer expectations. Effective feedback in customer service involves actively soliciting and listening to customer feedback, responding promptly to inquiries and concerns, and taking proactive steps to address issues and improve the overall customer experience.

Customer service feedback occurs through various channels, including surveys, feedback forms, social media, and direct interactions with customers. These channels provide organizations with valuable data and insights into customer perceptions, enabling them to make informed decisions and implement targeted improvements that drive customer satisfaction and loyalty.

Moreover, feedback in customer service is not limited to reactive measures; it also encompasses proactive initiatives to anticipate and address customer needs before they arise. By fostering a customer-centric mindset and culture, organizations can create positive experiences that resonate with customers and differentiate their brand in a competitive marketplace.

CHAPTER 5:

EFFECTIVE
FEEDBACK
TECHNIQUES

Feedback is only effective when delivered and received thoughtfully and intentionally. This chapter explores the art and science behind giving and receiving feedback, examining techniques and strategies that promote constructive communication and facilitate growth and development.

THE ART OF GIVING FEEDBACK

Giving feedback is an art that requires skill, empathy, and tact. Effective feedback is specific, actionable, and balanced. It focuses on behaviors rather than personal attributes, ensuring that individuals understand what actions they need to maintain or change. Moreover, effective feedback is delivered supportive, acknowledging individuals' efforts and providing encouragement and constructive criticism.

To give effective feedback, it is essential to be clear and concise, focusing on observable behaviors and their impact. Avoid generalizations or assumptions and provide specific examples to illustrate your points. Additionally, use non-judgmental and objective language, focusing on facts rather than opinions or interpretations.

Furthermore, effective feedback is timely and relevant and provided in a contextually appropriate manner. It is essential to consider the individual's readiness and receptiveness to feedback and choose an appropriate time and place for delivery. By delivering feedback with sensitivity and respect, you create an environment where individuals feel valued, supported, and motivated to improve.

COACHING CORNER

Story 1: The Code Review

In the bustling offices of Bye the Wave Technologies, a software development firm, Kevin was known for his sharp coding skills but also for his tendency to work independently, sometimes to the detriment of team cohesion. His manager, Laura, decided it was time to give him feedback after noticing some issues in his recent code review.

"Kevin, can we chat for a minute?" Laura asked after their weekly team stand-up.

"Sure, Laura," Kevin replied, slightly puzzled.

They moved to a quiet meeting room. Laura started with some positive feedback. "Kevin, your coding skills are top-notch, and your latest feature implementation is impressive. The efficiency improvements you made will save us a lot of processing time."

Kevin smiled, appreciating the recognition.

"However," Laura continued, "I noticed that your code reviews are often done in isolation, and sometimes, the rest of the team finds it hard to follow the changes without context. For instance, the recent update on the data handling module could have benefited from more comments and a brief explanation during the review meeting."

Kevin nodded, realizing the issue. "I guess I get so focused on the task that I forget to loop everyone in."

"I get it," Laura said with a supportive tone. "But remember, we work as a team. Providing clear comments in your code and a brief overview during meetings can help everyone stay on the same page and contribute more effectively. It's a small change that can make a big difference."

"Thanks, Laura. I'll make sure to do that from now on," Kevin said, feeling motivated to improve his collaborative efforts.

Laura's feedback was specific, actionable, and supportive. It helped Kevin understand how to enhance his teamwork skills while he felt valued and encouraged.

Story 2: The Sales Pitch

At Stewart Sales, a dynamic sales company, Rebecca, a junior sales representative, was enthusiastic and driven but sometimes struggled with her sales pitch delivery. Her supervisor, Tom, noticed this and decided to offer some feedback after a recent client meeting.

"Rebecca, can we have a quick chat in my office?" Tom asked.

"Of course, Tom," Rebecca replied, following him.

Once seated, Tom began. "Rebecca, your enthusiasm and drive are incredible. Your passion for our products really shines through."

Rebecca smiled, feeling proud.

"But" Tom continued, "during today's client meeting, I noticed that your pitch was a bit too fast-paced, and some key points were glossed over. For instance, when discussing the new product features, it seemed like the client needed more time to absorb the information."

Rebecca looked thoughtful. "I was trying to keep their attention, but I see what you mean."

"Exactly. It's important to balance enthusiasm with clarity. Pausing to emphasize key points and checking in with the client can ensure they're fully engaged and understand everything you're presenting," Tom suggested.

"I'll definitely work on that," Rebecca said, appreciative of the constructive advice.

Tom's feedback was clear, specific, and offered in a way that acknowledged Rebecca's strengths while providing actionable advice for improvement, fostering a supportive and developmental environment.

Story 3: The Design Feedback

In the creative studio of Vision Leads Designs, a graphic design firm, Daniel was a talented designer with a keen eye for detail. However, his designs sometimes failed to align with client expectations. His team leader, Maria, decided to give him feedback after a client review session.

"Daniel, do you have a few minutes to talk about the recent client feedback on the Johnson project?" Maria asked.

"Sure, Maria," Daniel replied, feeling a bit anxious.

They sat in a cozy corner of the studio. Maria started positively. "Daniel, your creativity is amazing, and the concepts you come up with are always unique and innovative."

Daniel relaxed a bit, feeling proud of his creativity.

"That said," Maria continued, "the client felt that the latest design didn't quite match their brand identity. For example, the color palette and typography were a bit too bold for their traditional brand image."

Daniel frowned slightly, realizing his oversight. "I was trying to make the design stand out, but I missed their brand's subtler tones."

"It's a fine line," Maria acknowledged. "To align more closely with their expectations, I suggest revisiting their brand guidelines and incorporating more of their classic elements while still adding your unique touch. Also, sharing drafts earlier for feedback could help ensure we're on the right track."

"That's a good idea. I'll do that in future projects," Daniel said, feeling supported and eager to improve.

Maria's feedback was specific, actionable, and empathetic. It helped Daniel understand how to better align his creative work with client expectations while allowing him to feel valued and encouraged in his role.

RECEIVING FEEDBACK

Receiving feedback requires openness and a willingness to learn. It involves actively listening to the feedback provider, suspending judgment, and reflecting on the insights gained. Effective feedback reception also involves seeking clarification, asking questions, and expressing gratitude for the feedback received.

To receive feedback effectively, it is essential to approach it with a growth mindset, viewing it as an opportunity for learning and improvement rather than a personal attack. Avoid becoming defensive or dismissive of feedback, and instead, focus on understanding the feedback provider's perspective and considering how you can apply the insights gained to enhance your performance.

Moreover, effective feedback reception involves taking ownership of your development and actively seeking growth opportunities. Use feedback as a catalyst for self-reflection and goal setting, identifying areas for improvement and developing action plans to address them. By embracing feedback with humility and openness, you create opportunities for personal and professional growth.

COACHING CORNER

Story 1: The Developer's Growth - A software development company

Ian was a junior developer at Techno Solutions, a software development firm. He had been working on a complex project and had just submitted his code for review. Tina, a senior developer, and Ian's mentor, was responsible for reviewing his work.

After reviewing the code, Tina called Ian into her office. "Ian, I've gone through your code, and there are a few things I'd like to discuss," she began.

Ian felt a twinge of anxiety but reminded himself to stay open. "Sure, Tim. I'm here to learn."

Tina started with some positive notes. "Your approach to solving the main algorithm was creative and efficient. Great job on that! However, I noticed a few areas where improvements are needed. For instance, your error handling is a bit sparse, and some redundant functions could be optimized."

Ian listened attentively, fighting the urge to defend his work. Instead, he asked, "Could you show me examples of the redundant functions and explain how I can improve the error handling?"

Tina appreciated Ian's willingness to learn and explain in detail, providing examples and suggesting resources for further reading.

"Thank you for this feedback, Tina. I see where I can improve and will work on these areas immediately," Ian said, genuinely grateful for the insights.

By receiving feedback with openness and a growth mindset, Ian was able to understand his areas for improvement and take actionable steps towards enhancing his skills. Subsequently, he regularly sought Tina's advice, using her feedback to refine his work continually.

Story 2: The Teacher's Reflection- Setting: An elementary school

Ellie was a new teacher at Greenfield Elementary. She was passionate about teaching but often found classroom management challenging. Mrs. Johnson, a seasoned teacher, observed one of Ellie's classes to provide feedback.

After the class, they sat down in the teachers' lounge. "Ellie, your lesson plan was well-structured, and the students were engaged with the activities," Mrs. Johnson began, offering initial praise.

Ellie smiled, but she knew there was more to come. "Thank you, Mrs. Johnson. I'm eager to hear your full thoughts."

"One area to consider is your classroom management. I noticed that when the students became a bit restless, it took a while to regain their attention. For instance, during the group activity, a few students were off-task, disrupting the lesson flow," Mrs. Johnson pointed out.

Ellie felt a bit defensive initially but took a deep breath. "I see. What strategies would you recommend improving in this area?"

Mrs. Johnson shared some techniques, such as using a clear signal for attention and incorporating more structured transitions between activities. She also suggested observing some of her classes for practical examples.

"Those are great suggestions. I'll try them out. Thank you for your feedback," Ellie said, noting the strategies.

By approaching feedback with an open mind and a desire to improve, Ellie gained valuable insights into her teaching methods. She applied the new strategies, and her classroom management skills improved significantly over time.

Story 3: The Sales Rep's Development - Setting: A sales company

Mike had been with Star Sales for a year and was eager to advance his career. However, his recent sales numbers have plateaued. Karen, his sales manager, scheduled a meeting to discuss his performance.

"Mike, I've reviewed your recent sales performance, and I wanted to share some feedback," Karen said as they sat in her office.

Mike nodded, ready to listen. "I appreciate any feedback that can help me improve."

"Your client relationships are strong, and you have a great rapport with them, which is a significant asset," Karen started. "However, I noticed that your closing rate has been lower than expected. For example, several deals stalled at the final stage in the last quarter."

Mike felt a bit defensive but knew Karen's feedback was meant to help. "I see. Can you pinpoint any specific areas where I might be going wrong?"

During the closing phase, Karen explained that Mike focused heavily on product details rather than addressing the client's emotional motivations and concerns. She suggested using more targeted questions to uncover client needs and incorporating storytelling techniques to make the final pitch more compelling.

"Those are insightful points. I hadn't considered the emotional aspect as much. Thank you for these tips," Mike said, appreciative of the guidance.

By receiving feedback openly and with a willingness to learn, Mike identified clear areas for improvement. He applied Karen's suggestions, refining his closing techniques and soon saw a marked improvement in his sales performance. This approach boosted his numbers and deepened his client relationships, paving the way for his career growth.

FEEDBACK MODELS AND FRAMEWORKS

Various models and frameworks provide structured approaches to delivering feedback effectively. These models help feedback providers organize their thoughts, clarify their intentions, and ensure that feedback is specific, actionable, and balanced.

One such model is SBI (Situation-Behavior-Impact), which involves describing the specific situation or behavior observed, explaining the impact of the behavior on oneself or others, and providing suggestions for improvement or reinforcement. This model ensures that feedback is focused on observable behaviors and their consequences, making it more actionable and relevant.

Another model is COIN (Context-Observation-Impact-Next steps), which incorporates additional elements such as providing context for the feedback, describing the observations made, explaining the impact of the behavior, and outlining the next steps for improvement. This model provides a more comprehensive framework for delivering feedback, ensuring that all relevant factors are considered and addressed.

Additionally, Pendleton's Rules provide a structured approach to feedback that involves individuals receiving feedback first, followed by self-assessment, feedback from others, and finally, an action plan for improvement. This model promotes self-reflection and accountability, empowering individuals to take ownership of their development and drive their own growth.

COACHING CORNER

Story: The Marketing Campaign Feedback - A marketing agency

Feedback Model Used: SBI (Situation-Behavior-Impact)

Lisa and Jack worked at Creations4Me Solutions, a marketing agency known for its innovative campaigns. Recently, Jack led a campaign for a major client, but there were some issues with its execution. Lisa decided to use the SBI model to provide structured feedback.

Situation: Lisa called Jack into her office for a feedback session. "Jack, let's talk about the recent campaign for our client, EcoHome. Specifically, I want to discuss the social media strategy you implemented last month."

Behavior: Lisa continued, "During the campaign, I observed that the posting schedule wasn't consistent. For example, there were gaps of several days without any posts, and multiple posts were made within a short period."

Impact: Lisa explained, "This inconsistency affected our engagement metrics. The client noticed a drop in interactions and reached out to express their concerns. Consistent posting is crucial for maintaining audience interest and engagement."

Jack nodded, recognizing the issue. "I see what you mean. I didn't realize the impact it had on our metrics."

Suggestions for Improvement: Lisa provided actionable advice. "To improve, I suggest creating a content calendar that outlines a balanced and consistent posting schedule. Additionally, scheduling posts using our social media management tools in advance can help maintain regularity."

Jack appreciated the structured feedback. "Thank you, Lisa. I'll implement these suggestions for the next campaign."

By using the SBI model, Lisa ensured her feedback was specific, actionable, and relevant, helping Jack understand the issue and providing clear steps for improvement.

Feedback Model Used: COIN (Context-Observation-Impact-Next steps)

Context: After a successful product launch, Karen, a sales manager at TechGear, wanted to provide feedback to Emily, a new sales representative, about her performance during the launch event.

"Emily, can we discuss your role in the recent product launch event for the new TechGear Smartwatch?" Karen began.

Observation: Karen continued, "I observed that during your product demonstration, you provided detailed technical explanations, which is great. However, some customers seemed a bit overwhelmed by the technical jargon."

Impact: Karen explained the consequences, "While your knowledge is impressive, the technical details appeared to confuse some potential buyers, and they might have missed understanding the core benefits of the product."

Emily listened carefully, realizing the importance of simplifying her language. "I didn't realize it was too technical for some customers."

Next Steps: Karen offered constructive advice. "For future demonstrations, try to focus on the product's main benefits and how it can improve customers' lives. Use simple, relatable language, and gauge the audience's reactions to adjust your level of detail accordingly."

Emily felt grateful for the comprehensive feedback. "Thanks, Karen. I'll definitely work on making my presentations more audience friendly."

Using the COIN model, Karen provided a thorough and balanced feedback session that covered all relevant aspects, ensuring Emily knew exactly what to work on for future improvements.

Feedback Model Used: Pendleton's Rules

Self-Assessment: At Health Group Clinic, Dr. Morgan, a senior physician, decided to give feedback to Dr. Lee, a junior physician, after a particularly challenging patient case. They began by discussing the case in a quiet meeting room.

"Dr. Lee, let's review Mr. Johnson's case," Dr. Morgan started. I'd like to hear your thoughts on how it went."

Dr. Lee reflected, "I think I managed the initial assessment well, but I struggled with the follow-up on his test results. I missed a critical lab result that delayed his diagnosis."

Feedback from Others: Dr. Morgan nodded. "I noticed that too. The initial assessment was thorough, but there was a delay in acting on the lab results, which impacted the patient's treatment timeline."

Action Plan: Dr. Morgan suggested, "To prevent this in the future, I recommend setting reminders for critical follow-ups in our patient management system. Also, perhaps consider a brief review with a colleague for complex cases to ensure nothing is overlooked."

Dr. Lee appreciated the constructive feedback and the opportunity for self-reflection. "Thank you, Dr. Morgan. I'll incorporate these strategies and be more vigilant with follow-ups."

Using Pendleton's Rules, Dr. Morgan provided a structured feedback session that encouraged self-assessment, peer feedback, and a clear action plan, empowering Dr. Lee to take ownership of his professional development.

These stories illustrate how different feedback models can be effectively applied in various professional contexts to provide structured, actionable, and balanced feedback, fostering a culture of continuous improvement and growth.

THE IMPORTANCE OF TIMING AND DELIVERY

Timing and delivery are crucial in feedback, as they can significantly impact how feedback is received and acted upon. Providing feedback at the right moment and in a constructive tone ensures that it is well-received and contributes to positive behavior change.

Choosing an appropriate time and place for delivering feedback is essential, as well as ensuring that the individual is receptive and emotionally prepared to receive it. Avoid delivering feedback in high-stress or emotionally charged situations, which can lead to defensiveness or resistance.

Furthermore, pay attention to your tone and language when delivering feedback, ensuring it is supportive, respectful, and non-judgmental. Use language that is clear and specific, avoiding ambiguity or vague statements. Additionally, provide feedback in a manner that is consistent with the individual's preferred communication style, taking into account their cultural background and personal preferences.

Paying attention to timing and delivery creates an environment where feedback is valued and constructive communication flourishes. Effective feedback promotes trust, respect, and collaboration, fostering a culture of continuous improvement and growth.

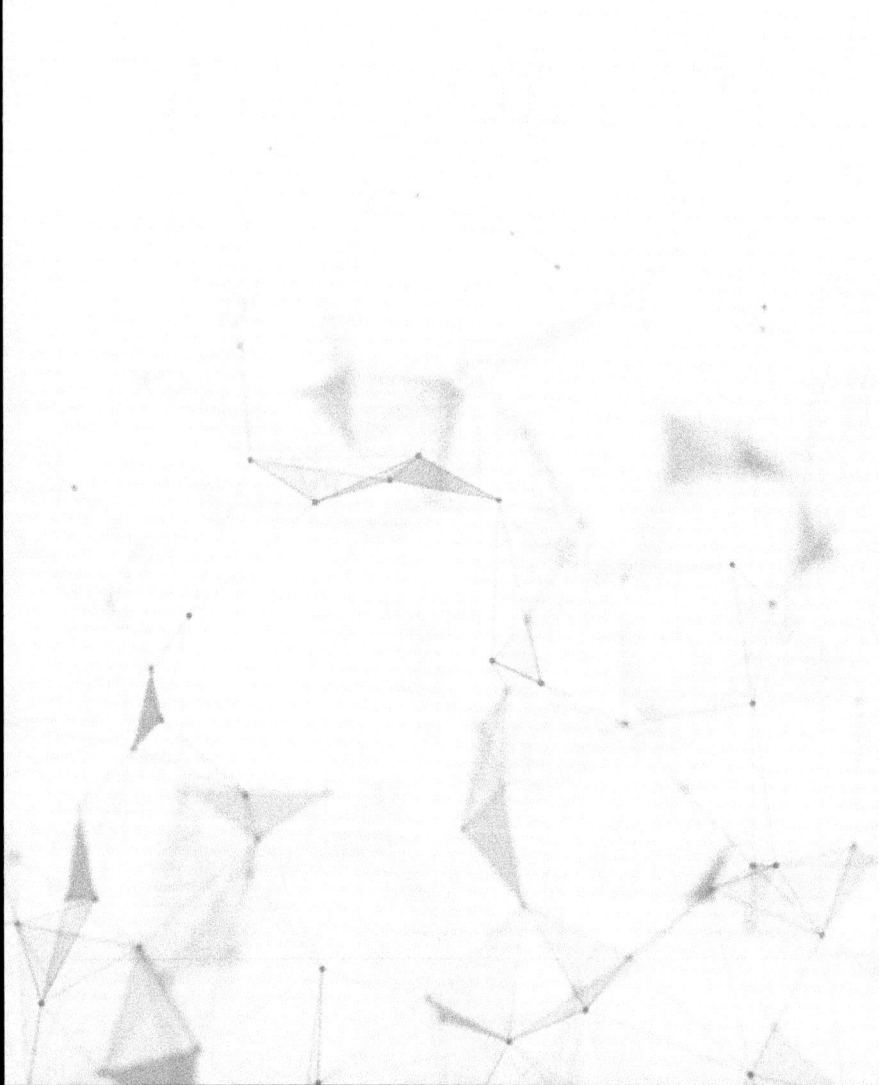

CHAPTER 6:

OVERCOMING CHALLENGES IN FEEDBACK

Despite its importance, feedback can be fraught with challenges that hinder its effectiveness. In this chapter, we explore common obstacles encountered in the feedback process and provide strategies for overcoming them to promote constructive communication and growth.

DEALING WITH NEGATIVE REACTIONS

Negative reactions to feedback are a natural part of the feedback process. When receiving feedback that challenges their beliefs or behaviors, individuals may feel defensive, frustrated, or even resentful. Addressing these reactions requires empathy, clarity, and a focus on positive outcomes.

When encountering negative reactions to feedback, it is essential to approach the situation with empathy and understanding. Acknowledge the individual's feelings and concerns and reassure them that feedback is intended to support their growth and development rather than criticize their abilities. By clarifying the specific behaviors or actions that prompted the feedback and highlighting the potential benefits of making positive changes, you can counter negative reactions to feedback.

Moreover, focus on solutions rather than dwelling on the problem. Encourage the individual to view feedback as an opportunity for learning and improvement and work together to develop actionable steps for addressing areas of concern. By fostering a supportive and collaborative environment, you can help individuals overcome negative reactions to feedback and embrace it as a catalyst for growth.

COACHING CORNER

Story 1: The Designer's Frustration - A graphic design firm

Emma, a talented graphic designer at All Star Creations, had just completed a major project for a high-profile client. Mark, the creative director, had some feedback on her work, which he knew might be challenging for Emma to hear.

"Emma, can we discuss your recent project for BriteTech?" Mark asked gently.

Emma nodded, though she felt a knot in her stomach.

"Your designs are innovative and visually striking," Mark began. "However, the client felt that the branding elements weren't consistently represented throughout the materials. For example, the color scheme in the brochures didn't align with their brand guidelines."

Emma's face tightened with frustration. "But I thought adding those colors would make the design stand out more!"

Mark noticed her defensiveness and responded with empathy. "I understand why you made those choices; your creativity is one of your strongest assets. The feedback isn't about your talent but aligning with the client's expectations. They have specific guidelines that need to be followed closely."

Emma sighed, still feeling upset. "It feels like they're stifling creativity."

Mark nodded sympathetically. "It can feel that way but think of it as a challenge to creatively work within the constraints. It's an opportunity to show you can innovate while meeting client needs. Let's review their guidelines and see how we can adapt your designs without losing your unique touch."

Emma appreciated Mark's supportive approach. "Okay, let's do that. I want to make it right."

By acknowledging Emma's feelings and focusing on solutions, Mark helped her shift her perspective and embrace the feedback as a growth opportunity.

Story 2: The Sales Representative's Defensiveness - A sales company

John, a sales representative at Appex Sales, had recently received feedback from a key client about his sales pitch. Zi, his sales manager, needed to address this with him.

"Zack, do you have a moment to discuss the feedback from your last client meeting?" ZI asked.

Zack frowned. "Sure, but I think I did everything right."

Zi began carefully. "The client appreciated your enthusiasm and product knowledge. However, they felt you didn't listen enough to their needs and concerns. They mentioned that they felt rushed during the meeting."

Zack's defensiveness kicked in. "I was trying to be efficient and cover all the points. They didn't seem to have any specific questions at the time."

Zi acknowledged his feelings. "I understand your intention to be thorough and efficient. It's clear you're very committed to your role. Sometimes though, clients need more space to express their concerns and feel heard."

Zack still seemed frustrated. "But I followed the script we practiced."

Zi offered clarity and support. "Scripts are helpful, but flexibility is key. Asking open-ended questions and giving the client time to respond can create a more engaging conversation. How about we practice some techniques to balance providing information and listening?"

Zack took a deep breath. "Okay, I'm willing to try that."

By empathizing with Zack and focusing on practical solutions, Zi helped him overcome his defensiveness and see feedback as an opportunity to improve his client interactions.

Story 3: The Teacher's Resentment - An elementary school

Mr. Smith, a dedicated teacher at Maplewood Elementary, had received some critical feedback from parents about his classroom management. Mrs. Taylor, the principal, needed to discuss this with him.

"Mr. Smith, can we talk about some concerns raised by the parents in your class?" Mrs. Taylor asked.

Mr. Smith sighed, feeling a wave of resentment. "Sure, but I don't see what the problem is. I'm doing my best."

Mrs. Taylor started with empathy. "I know you're working hard and care deeply about your students. The feedback isn't about questioning your dedication. Parents are concerned that some students struggle to stay focused and engaged."

Mr. Smith's resentment showed. "They don't understand what it's like to manage a classroom. It's not easy."

Mrs. Taylor acknowledged his feelings. "You're right; teaching is incredibly challenging, and your efforts are valued. The feedback is meant to help you address specific issues, not criticize your abilities. For example, some students struggle to follow along during group activities. Perhaps incorporating more structured activities and clear instructions could help."

Mr. Smith felt slightly calmer but still defensive. "I feel like they're always complaining."

Mrs. Taylor reassured him. "It's natural to feel that way but think of this as an opportunity to enhance your teaching strategies. Let's work together to find some techniques that can make the classroom environment more manageable for you and more engaging for the students."

Mr. Smith took a deep breath. "Alright, I'm willing to try some new methods."

By showing empathy, providing clarity, and focusing on positive outcomes, Mrs. Taylor helped Mr. Smith overcome his initial resentment and see the feedback as a chance to improve his teaching approach.

NAVIGATING CULTURAL DIFFERENCES

Cultural differences can significantly impact how feedback is perceived and delivered. Different cultural norms, communication styles, and attitudes towards authority can influence individuals' receptiveness to feedback and their willingness to provide candid input.

To navigate cultural differences effectively, it is essential to understand and respect each individual's cultural background and communication preferences. Take the time to learn about cultural norms and expectations regarding feedback in diverse cultural contexts and adapt your approach accordingly.

Moreover, this learning fosters open communication and dialogue about cultural differences to promote mutual understanding and respect. Encourage individuals to share their perspectives and experiences and be receptive to feedback on your own communication style and behavior.

By embracing cultural diversity and inclusivity in feedback practices, you create an environment where individuals feel valued, respected, and empowered to contribute their unique perspectives and insights.

COACHING CORNER

Story 1: The Global Marketing Team - A multinational marketing firm

Mila, the American team lead at Global Marketing, was conducting a performance review meeting with her diverse team members: Hiroshi, Maria, and Ahmed. Each came from a different cultural background, and Mila knew she had to navigate these differences carefully to provide effective feedback.

Mila started with Hiroshi. "Hiroshi, your attention to detail in the market analysis is impressive. However, I noticed that your reports often lack direct recommendations. Can you provide more actionable insights in the future?"

Hiroshi, whose Japanese cultural norm avoids direct criticism and values group harmony, nodded politely. "I will try to be more specific in my recommendations."

Mila then turned to Maria. "Maria, your creative content has been engaging our audience very well. However, there have been some instances where the posts did not align with our brand guidelines. Could you please double-check the guidelines before publishing?"

Maria, from a culture that values expressive communication and personal relationships, responded enthusiastically. "Thank you for the feedback, Mila! I'll make sure to review the guidelines more carefully."

Finally, Mila addressed Ahmed. "Ahmed, your data analysis skills are top-notch, and your insights have been invaluable. I'd like to see you participate more actively in team meetings and share your thoughts."

Ahmed hesitated, coming from a culture that often shows respect by deferring to authority. "I appreciate the feedback. I will try to contribute more in meetings."

After the meeting, Mila reflected on the reactions and decided to foster a more open dialogue about cultural differences.

She scheduled a team-building session where each member could share their cultural norms and preferences regarding feedback.

During the session, Hiroshi explained that feedback is often given indirectly to maintain harmony in Japan. Maria shared that in Brazil, feedback is more informal and personal. Ahmed mentioned that in Egypt, it's common to show respect by not challenging authority openly.

By understanding these cultural nuances, Mila adapted her feedback approach. She gave Hiroshi more detailed written feedback to respect his preference for indirect communication. She ensured her feedback to Maria was clear but warm, aligning with her expressive style. For Ahmed, she created a more inclusive environment where he felt comfortable sharing his ideas.

Through these adjustments, Mila fostered a culture of respect and inclusivity, allowing each team member to feel valued and empowered.

Story 2: The Engineering Project - An international engineering firm

Sarah, a British project manager at Innovate Tech Engineering, led a team of engineers from various cultural backgrounds. She needed to navigate these differences to deliver effective feedback and ensure the project's success.

Sarah began by addressing Liu. "Liu, your technical skills are exceptional, and your designs are always precise. However, I've noticed that you often avoid direct confrontation in meetings, which sometimes leads to unresolved issues."

Liu, aware of the Chinese cultural norm of maintaining face and avoiding direct conflict, nodded. "I understand. I will try to address issues more directly."

Next, Sarah spoke to Carlos. "Carlos, your problem-solving abilities are fantastic, and you bring great energy to the team.

Sometimes, though, your enthusiasm can come across as interrupting others. Can you be mindful of giving others a chance to speak?"

Carlos, from a culture that values expressive and direct communication, smiled. "Sure, Sarah. I'll make sure to listen more."

Lastly, Sarah addressed Aisha. "Aisha, your contributions to the electrical design are very valuable. I'd like to see you take on a more leadership role within the team."

Aisha, coming from a culture that often emphasizes collective success and respect for hierarchy, hesitated. "Thank you, Sarah. I will try to step up more."

To better understand her team, Sarah organized a cultural exchange workshop. Liu explained that in China, it's important to avoid public criticism to save face. Carlos shared that in Mexico, conversations are lively and interruptions are seen as a sign of engagement. Aisha mentioned that in Nigeria, leadership is often shown through collaboration rather than assertiveness.

With these insights, Sarah adjusted her feedback style. She provided Liu with private, written feedback to respect his cultural preferences. She gave Carlos clear but friendly reminders to allow others to speak. Aisha encouraged collaborative leadership opportunities and provided more public recognition.

By adapting her approach, Sarah created a more inclusive and effective team dynamic, respecting each member's cultural background and communication style.

Story 3: The Software Development Team - Setting: A tech startup

John, a Canadian team lead at Tek Solutions, managed a diverse software development team. He knew navigating cultural differences was crucial for effective feedback and team cohesion.

John started with Priya. "Priya, your coding skills are excellent, and you always meet deadlines. However, I've noticed that you rarely ask for help, even when facing challenges."

Priya, aware of the Indian cultural norm of respecting hierarchy and showing self-reliance, nodded. "I'll try to ask for help more often when needed."

Next, John addressed Alexei. "Alexei, your attention to detail in QA is outstanding. However, the team can sometimes perceive your direct communication style as harsh."

Alexei, from a culture that values directness and blunt feedback, shrugged. "I'll try to soften my approach."

Finally, John spoke to Fatima. "Fatima, your designs are always user-friendly and creative. I'd like to see you participate more actively in brainstorming sessions."

Coming from a culture that often values modesty and respect for authority, Fatima hesitated. "I will try to contribute more."

John realized the need for a more inclusive approach and organized a cultural awareness session. Priya explained that asking for help can be seen as a sign of weakness in India. Alexei shared that in Russia, direct feedback is considered honest and straightforward. Fatima mentioned that modesty and deference to authority are valued in Saudi Arabia.

With this understanding, John adapted his feedback style. He encouraged Priya to view seeking help as a collaborative effort. He worked with Alexei to find a balance between honesty and tact. For Fatima, he created a safe space for her to share ideas without fear of overstepping.

By embracing these cultural differences, John fostered a supportive and respectful team environment, enhancing collaboration and performance.

Story 4: The Customer Service Team - A Global Customer Service Center

Maria, a Spanish manager at a global customer service center, led a team with diverse cultural backgrounds. She needed to navigate these differences to provide effective feedback and improve team performance.

Maria began with Kenji. "Kenji, your politeness and thoroughness in handling customer queries are commendable. However, your responses can sometimes be too detailed, leading to longer call times."

Kenji nodded, aware of the Japanese cultural norm of providing comprehensive service. "I understand. I will try to be more concise."

Next, Maria addressed Lila. "Lila, your efficiency and directness are great for resolving issues quickly. However, some customers feel that your tone can be too abrupt."

Lila, from a culture that values direct and clear communication, responded. "I'll try to be more mindful of my tone."

Lastly, Maria spoke to Raj. "Raj, customers appreciate your friendly and empathetic approach. I'd like to see you focus more on resolving issues within the first call."

Raj, aware of the Indian cultural norm of building relationships, nodded. "I'll work on being more solution oriented."

Maria organized a cultural competency workshop to understand her team better. Kenji explained that in Japan, thoroughness is a sign of respect and quality service. Lila shared that in France, direct communication is valued for its clarity. Raj mentioned that in India, building a rapport with customers is key to good service.

With these insights, Maria adjusted her feedback approach. She encouraged Kenji to balance thoroughness with efficiency. She helped Lila find ways to maintain directness while softening her tone. For Raj, she provided strategies to resolve issues efficiently while maintaining his friendly approach.

Maria created a more inclusive and effective feedback environment by understanding and respecting cultural differences, enhancing team performance and customer satisfaction.

ADDRESSING COMMON MISCONCEPTIONS

Misconceptions about feedback, such as seeing it as criticism or a sign of failure, can hinder its effectiveness and create barriers to communication. Educating individuals about feedback's true purpose and value is essential for overcoming these misconceptions.

Firstly, clarify the distinction between feedback and criticism. While criticism focuses on fault-finding and blame, feedback is intended to provide constructive guidance and support for improvement. Emphasize that feedback is not a reflection of one's worth or competence but rather an opportunity for growth and development.

Additionally, it debunks common myths about feedback, such as the belief that only negative feedback is valuable or that feedback should be avoided to prevent hurt feelings. Highlight the benefits of feedback in promoting learning, enhancing performance, and fostering meaningful connections.

Addressing common misconceptions and promoting a positive mindset towards feedback creates an environment where individuals feel empowered to give and receive feedback openly and constructively.

FEEDBACK FATIGUE AND HOW TO AVOID IT

Feedback fatigue occurs when individuals feel overwhelmed by constant feedback, leading to burnout and diminished effectiveness. To avoid feedback fatigue, it is essential to balance the frequency and quality of feedback and ensure that it is relevant and meaningful.

Encourage individuals to prioritize actionable and relevant feedback to their goals and development areas. Avoid overwhelming them with excessive or unnecessary feedback, and focus on providing specific, timely, and constructive feedback.

Moreover, it promotes a feedback culture that emphasizes quality over quantity and encourages open communication and dialogue. Encourage individuals to seek feedback selectively and to prioritize opportunities for reflection and self-assessment.

By fostering a balanced approach to feedback and promoting a supportive and empowering feedback culture, you can help individuals avoid feedback fatigue and maintain its effectiveness as a tool for growth and development.

CHAPTER 7

FEEDBACK AND PERSONAL GROWTH

Feedback serves as a powerful catalyst for personal growth and development. In this chapter, we explore how individuals can harness the transformative power of feedback to cultivate self-improvement, set meaningful goals, build resilience, and foster a growth mindset.

USING FEEDBACK FOR SELF-IMPROVEMENT

Feedback is a valuable tool for self-improvement, providing individuals with valuable insights into their strengths, weaknesses, and areas for development. By actively seeking and embracing feedback, individuals can gain a deeper understanding of their performance and behaviors, identify areas for improvement, and take proactive steps toward personal growth.

Effective feedback serves as a mirror, reflecting individuals' actions and behaviors and offering guidance for improvement. By embracing feedback with humility and openness, individuals can leverage it as a catalyst for self-reflection and continuous improvement. Whether in the workplace, educational setting, or personal relationships, feedback allows individuals to refine their skills, overcome challenges, and reach their full potential.

USING FEEDBACK FOR SELF-IMPROVEMENT: A DETAILED GUIDE

Feedback is a powerful tool for self-improvement, offering individuals critical insights into their strengths, weaknesses, and areas for development. By actively seeking and embracing feedback, individuals can gain a deeper understanding of their performance and behaviors, identify areas for improvement, and take proactive steps toward personal growth. Here's a detailed example of how to operationalize this concept:

Step 1: Establish a Feedback-Friendly Environment

- Objective: Create an environment where feedback is seen as a positive and integral part of personal and professional development.

- Actions: Normalize Feedback: Encourage regular feedback sessions and integrate feedback into the daily routine. Make it a norm to ask for and give feedback in meetings, during projects, and in casual conversations.

- Build Trust: Foster a culture of trust where individuals feel safe giving and receiving honest feedback. This can be achieved by demonstrating respect, confidentiality, and support.

- Provide Training: Offer training sessions on effectively giving and receiving feedback. Teach employees the principles of constructive feedback and active listening.

Step 2: Actively Seek Feedback

- Objective: Encourage individuals to take the initiative in seeking feedback from various sources.

- Actions: 360-Degree Feedback: Implement a 360-degree feedback system where individuals receive feedback from peers, supervisors, and subordinates. This provides a well-rounded view of their performance.

- Regular Check-Ins: Schedule regular one-on-one meetings with supervisors or mentors to discuss performance and areas for improvement.

- Anonymous Surveys: Use anonymous surveys to collect candid feedback, especially if individuals are hesitant to provide direct feedback.

Step 3: Embrace Feedback with Humility and Openness

- Objective: Foster an attitude of humility and openness towards feedback, viewing it as an opportunity for growth rather than criticism.

- Actions: Active Listening: When receiving feedback, listen actively without interrupting. Focus on understanding the message rather than preparing a defense.

- Acknowledge and Reflect: Acknowledge the feedback received and take time to reflect on it. Consider how the feedback aligns with personal perceptions and experiences.

- Ask Clarifying Questions: If the feedback is unclear, ask for specific examples or further clarification to fully understand the points being made.

Step 4: Analyze and Prioritize Feedback

- Objective: Analyze the feedback to identify key areas for improvement and prioritize actions.

- Actions: Identify Patterns: Look for recurring themes or patterns in the feedback to pinpoint specific strengths and areas for development.

- Set Priorities: Prioritize feedback based on its impact on performance and personal goals. Focus on areas that will make the most significant difference.

- Create an Action Plan: Develop a structured action plan to address the prioritized feedback. Set specific, measurable, achievable, relevant, and time-bound (SMART) goals.

Step 5: Implement Changes and Monitor Progress

- Objective: Take proactive steps to implement changes based on feedback and monitor progress over time.

- Actions: Implement Changes: Start with small, manageable changes and gradually build on them. This could include adopting new behaviors, learning new skills, or altering task approaches.

- Seek Support: Engage a mentor, coach, or peer to provide ongoing support and accountability.

- Monitor Progress: Review progress toward the action plan's goals regularly. Adjust the plan as needed based on new feedback and experiences.

Step 6: Reflect and Iterate

- Objective: Use feedback as a continuous loop for ongoing self-improvement.

- Actions: Reflect Regularly: Set aside time for regular self-reflection to evaluate the impact of the changes and identify new improvement areas.

- Seek Feedback on Improvements: Ask for feedback on the changes implemented to ensure they are effective and make necessary adjustments.

- Iterate and Improve: Treat feedback as an ongoing process. Continuously seek, embrace, and act on feedback to foster perpetual growth and development.

Example in Practice: A Workplace Scenario

Scenario: Jai, a project manager, wants to improve her leadership skills.

- Establish a Feedback-Friendly Environment: Jane's organization encourages a culture of open feedback. Jai's team holds regular meetings where feedback is a standard agenda item.

- Actively Seek Feedback: Jai requests 360-degree feedback from her team, peers, and supervisor. She also uses an anonymous survey to gather candid insights.

- Embrace Feedback with Humility and Openness: Jai receives feedback that she could improve her delegation skills. She listens actively, acknowledges the feedback, and reflects on her current delegation practices.

- Analyze and Prioritize Feedback: Jai identifies delegation as a key area for improvement. She sets a SMART goal to delegate more effectively by assigning tasks based on team members' strengths and providing clear instructions.

- Implement Changes and Monitor Progress: Jai starts delegating more strategically and seeks regular feedback from her team to ensure effective changes. She also checks in with her mentor for additional guidance.

- Reflect and Iterate: Jai reflects on the feedback and notices improved team performance and satisfaction. She continues to seek feedback to refine her delegation skills and identify new areas for growth.

By operationalizing feedback for self-improvement, individuals like Jai can continuously refine their skills, overcome challenges, and reach their full potential, ultimately benefiting both themselves and their organizations.

SETTING GOALS BASED ON FEEDBACK

Setting goals based on feedback ensures that efforts are focused on areas that need improvement, providing individuals with a clear path for growth and development. Feedback helps individuals identify areas where they can make meaningful progress and set SMART (Specific, Measurable, Achievable, Relevant, Time-bound) goals that align with their aspirations and aspirations.

By incorporating feedback into the goal-setting process, individuals can ensure that their efforts are directed towards areas of highest impact. Feedback serves as a compass, guiding individuals towards areas where they can make the most significant improvements and achieve their desired outcomes. Moreover, setting goals based on feedback gives individuals a sense of purpose and direction, motivating them to take action and pursue their aspirations with determination and perseverance.

Setting SMART Goals: An example

Based on the feedback, Jane and her manager collaboratively set the following SMART goals to help her make meaningful progress:

Specific:

* Goal: Improve project management skills by completing a project management course and applying learned techniques to current campaigns.

* Details: Jane will enroll in an online project management course that covers time management, task prioritization, and team coordination.

Measurable:

* Goal: Complete the project management course with a minimum score of 80% and apply at least three new project management techniques to her current work.

* Details: Jane will track her progress through course assessments and implement new techniques in her upcoming campaigns, documenting their impact on efficiency and outcomes.

Achievable:

* Goal: Manage at least three marketing campaigns simultaneously and maintain deadlines and maintain quality.

* Details: Jane will gradually take on more projects, starting with two campaigns and then progressing to three, ensuring she applies the new techniques effectively.

Relevant:

* Goal: Enhance project management skills to better align with the company's objectives of increasing productivity and delivering high-quality campaigns on time.

* Details: Improved project management will help Jane contribute more effectively to the team's goals, ensuring campaigns are executed smoothly and efficiently.

Time-bound:

- Goal: Complete the project management course within three months and demonstrate improved project management skills in the next six months.

- Details: Jane will enroll in the course within the next two weeks, complete it by the end of three months, and apply her new skills over the following three months, with regular check-ins with her manager.

Monitoring Progress and Adjusting Goals

- Jane and her manager schedule bi-weekly meetings to discuss her progress, challenges, and successes. These check-ins allow for adjustments to the goals if necessary and provide continuous support and feedback to ensure Jane stays on track.

First Check-in:

- Manager: "Hi Jane, how is the project management course going?"

- Jane: "It's going well. I've completed the first module on time management and have started implementing some techniques in my current projects."

Subsequent Check-ins:

- Manager: "Great to hear! Let's discuss how these new techniques impact your work and what adjustments we can make to further support your progress."

By setting SMART goals based on the feedback received, Jane can make meaningful progress in her professional development, aligning her efforts with her aspirations and the company's objectives. This structured approach ensures that her goals are clear, achievable, and focused on continuous improvement.

BUILDING RESILIENCE THROUGH FEEDBACK

Resilience is built by embracing feedback, learning from it, and persevering despite challenges. Feedback serves as a catalyst for resilience-building, providing individuals with opportunities to adapt, grow, and thrive in the face of adversity.

By embracing feedback with an open mind and a positive attitude, individuals can develop resilience and overcome setbacks with grace and resilience. Feedback helps individuals develop the resilience to bounce back from failures, setbacks, and criticism, enabling them to persevere in pursuing their goals and aspirations.

Moreover, feedback fosters a growth mindset, which views challenges as opportunities for learning and growth rather than insurmountable obstacles. By adopting a growth mindset, individuals can cultivate resilience, develop coping strategies, and thrive in the face of adversity.

DEVELOPING A GROWTH MINDSET

A growth mindset views feedback as an opportunity for improvement rather than a judgment. It encourages individuals to embrace challenges, learn from failures, and persist in pursuing their goals and aspirations. By adopting a growth mindset, individuals can develop the resilience, determination, and perseverance needed to overcome obstacles and succeed.

Feedback plays a crucial role in fostering a growth mindset by providing individuals with opportunities for learning and development. By embracing feedback with humility and openness, individuals can cultivate a growth mindset and approach challenges confidently and optimistically.

Moreover, a growth mindset encourages individuals to take ownership of their learning and development, seek feedback, and actively seek opportunities for growth and improvement.

By embracing a growth mindset, individuals can unlock their full potential and achieve their aspirations with passion, purpose, and resilience.

CHAPTER 8:

BUILDING A FEEDBACK CULTURE

Creating a culture of feedback is essential for fostering open communication, driving continuous improvement, and nurturing a supportive environment where individuals can thrive. This chapter explores strategies for building a feedback culture within organizations, emphasizing the importance of leadership, training, and continuous improvement through feedback loops.

CREATING AN ENVIRONMENT THAT ENCOURAGES FEEDBACK

A feedback culture is rooted in creating an environment where open communication and continuous improvement are valued and encouraged. It involves cultivating safe spaces where individuals feel comfortable sharing their thoughts, ideas, and concerns without fear of judgment or reprisal.

Organizations must prioritize transparency, trust, and respect in their interactions to create a feedback culture. Leaders should lead by example, demonstrating a willingness to give and receive feedback openly and constructively. Moreover, organizations should recognize and celebrate feedback, highlighting its role in driving growth and innovation.

By fostering an environment where feedback is valued and sought after, organizations can create a culture of continuous improvement that helps individuals feel empowered to contribute their insights and ideas.

STRATEGY PLAN FOR LEADERS: BUILDING A FEEDBACK CULTURE

1. Establish a Foundation of Trust and Transparency

Objective: Create an environment where open communication and continuous improvement are valued and encouraged.

Actions:

Lead by Example: Demonstrate a willingness to give and receive feedback openly and constructively. Share personal experiences of how feedback has helped you grow.

Communicate Purpose: Clearly articulate the purpose and benefits of feedback to all team members. Emphasize that feedback is aimed at growth and improvement, not criticism.

Build Trust: Establish trust by being consistent, fair, and respectful in all interactions. Ensure that feedback is given in a supportive and non-judgmental manner.

Encourage Openness: Foster a culture where employees feel safe to share their thoughts, ideas, and concerns without fear of judgment or reprisal.

Metrics for Success:

Increase in the number of feedback interactions between team members and leaders.

Employee surveys indicate higher levels of trust and openness.

2. Provide Training and Resources

Objective: Equip all team members with the skills and tools to effectively give and receive feedback.

Actions:

Feedback Training Workshops: Conduct regular workshops on effective feedback techniques, such as the SBI

(Situation-Behavior-Impact) model and the DESC (Describe-Express-Specify-Consequences) script.

Role-Playing Exercises: Use role-playing exercises to practice giving and receiving feedback in a safe and controlled environment.

Resource Library: Create a resource library with articles, books, and videos on feedback best practices.

Mentorship Programs: Pair employees with mentors who can provide ongoing feedback and guidance.

Metrics for Success:

Attendance and participation rates in feedback training workshops.

Improvement in feedback quality as assessed through peer reviews and supervisor evaluations.

3. Integrate Feedback into Daily Operations

Objective: Make feedback a regular and integral part of the organizational workflow.

Actions:

Regular Check-Ins: Schedule one-on-one meetings between employees and supervisors to discuss performance, goals, and feedback.

Team Feedback Sessions: Hold regular team meetings where feedback is a standing agenda item. Encourage team members to share constructive insights on projects and processes.

360-Degree Feedback: Implement a 360-degree feedback system where employees receive feedback from peers, subordinates, and supervisors.

Feedback Tools: Utilize digital tools and platforms to facilitate continuous feedback. Implement feedback apps or software that allow for real-time feedback exchanges.

Metrics for Success:

The frequency of feedback interactions was recorded in the feedback tools.

Employee feedback indicates satisfaction with the regularity and quality of feedback received.

4. Recognize and Celebrate Feedback

Objective: Highlight the role of feedback in driving growth and innovation, and recognize those who contribute valuable insights.

Actions:

Feedback Recognition Programs: Establish programs to recognize and reward employees actively participating in the feedback process and contributing valuable insights.

Celebrate Success Stories: Share success stories of individuals or teams who have benefited from feedback, showcasing the positive impact of a feedback culture.

Public Acknowledgement: Regularly acknowledge and thank employees for their feedback during team meetings, company-wide communications, and performance reviews.

Metrics for Success: Number of employees recognized for their feedback contributions. Employee engagement scores related to feeling valued and heard.

5. Continuously Improve Through Feedback Loops

Objective: Use feedback to drive continuous improvement at both the individual and organizational levels.

Actions:

Feedback Loops: Establish feedback loops where feedback is reviewed, acted upon, and followed up. Ensure that feedback results in actionable plans and measurable outcomes.

Track Progress: Monitor progress on feedback-driven initiatives and provide updates to the team. Use metrics and KPIs to assess the impact of feedback on performance.

Iterate and Adapt: Encourage a mindset of continuous improvement by regularly revisiting feedback processes and making necessary adjustments based on employee input and organizational needs.

Metrics for Success:

Implementation rate of feedback-driven changes.

Measurable improvements in key performance indicators (KPIs) as a result of feedback initiatives.

By following this strategy plan, leaders can create a thriving organizational feedback culture. Prioritizing trust, transparency, and respect, providing comprehensive training, integrating feedback into daily operations, recognizing contributions, and establishing continuous improvement loops will empower individuals and teams to embrace feedback as a catalyst for growth and innovation. By strategically applying these principles, organizations can unlock their full potential and foster a culture of continuous improvement.

LEADERSHIP AND FEEDBACK

Leaders play a crucial role in fostering a feedback culture within organizations. They set the tone by modeling feedback behaviors and demonstrating a commitment to open communication and continuous improvement.

Effective leaders prioritize feedback as a personal and professional growth tool, providing regular opportunities for individuals to share their thoughts, ideas, and concerns. They create a supportive environment where feedback is encouraged, valued, and acted upon promptly.

Moreover, leaders should actively seek feedback from their teams, demonstrating humility and a willingness to learn and grow. By fostering a culture of openness and transparency, leaders can create an environment where individuals feel empowered to give and receive feedback openly and constructively.

COACHING CORNER

Story 1: Transforming Team Dynamics through Feedback

Background: Emma, a new team leader at a marketing agency, inherited a team with low morale and poor performance. The previous leader had rarely given feedback, and when they did, it could have been more constructive. Emma recognized the need to change the team's dynamics and decided to prioritize creating a feedback culture.

Action: Emma started by holding a team meeting to discuss the importance of feedback and how it could drive personal and professional growth. She introduced regular one-on-one check-ins, where she provided constructive feedback using the SBI (Situation-Behavior-Impact) model. She encouraged her team to share their thoughts and concerns openly during these sessions.

Emma also implemented weekly team feedback sessions where everyone could provide feedback on ongoing projects. She created an anonymous feedback system for those who felt uncomfortable giving feedback directly. To build trust, Emma consistently acted on her feedback, making necessary adjustments and communicating the changes to the team.

Outcome: Within a few months, team morale and performance improved significantly. Team members felt valued and heard, and their confidence in sharing ideas and feedback increased. The open feedback culture led to innovative solutions and more efficient workflows. Emma's willingness to seek feedback from her team demonstrated her humility and commitment to continuous improvement. The team's success became a case study in the agency, showcasing the transformative power of a feedback culture.

Story 2: Enhancing Innovation through Constructive Insights

Background: David, the CEO of a tech startup, noticed that his company's innovation rate had plateaued. Despite having a talented team, employees seemed hesitant to take risks or share new ideas. David realized the company lacked a strong feedback culture that encouraged open communication and constructive insights.

Action: David introduced a series of initiatives to foster a feedback culture. He started with a company-wide meeting to emphasize the value of feedback and innovation. He implemented bi-weekly innovation labs where teams could present their projects and receive constructive insights from their peers. David encouraged the use of the DESC (Describe-Express-Specify-Consequences) script to provide clear and actionable feedback.

To set an example, David openly sought feedback from his team during town hall meetings and one-on-one sessions. He showed his commitment to learning by acting on his feedback and sharing his personal growth journey with the company. Additionally, David established a recognition program to celebrate employees who provided valuable feedback and innovative ideas.

Outcome: The startup experienced a surge in innovation, with new product ideas and improvements flowing regularly. Employees felt more empowered to take risks and share their insights, knowing their feedback was valued and acted upon. The open communication and continuous improvement culture led to a stronger, more cohesive team. David's leadership in modeling feedback behaviors and prioritizing constructive insights transformed the company's approach to innovation.

Story 3: Building Trust and Transparency Through Feedback

Background: Sophia, a senior manager at a large manufacturing firm, faced challenges with employee engagement and trust. The firm's hierarchical structure made employees hesitant to share feedback, fearing negative repercussions. Sophia understood that building a feedback culture was essential for improving engagement and trust.

Action: Sophia initiated a series of changes to create a more open and transparent feedback culture. She started by holding listening sessions with employees at all levels to understand their concerns and gather initial feedback. She then introduced regular feedback training workshops to equip employees with the skills to give and receive feedback effectively.

Sophia implemented a 360-degree feedback system, ensuring that feedback flowed in all directions, not just top-down. She held monthly town hall meetings where she shared updates on actions taken based on employee feedback, demonstrating transparency and accountability. To further build trust, Sophia encouraged leaders at all levels to share their own experiences with feedback and personal growth.

Outcome: Employee engagement and trust improved markedly. The feedback culture fostered by Sophia led to more open communication, greater collaboration, and a sense of shared purpose. Employees felt more comfortable sharing their ideas and concerns, knowing their feedback would be taken seriously and acted upon. Sophia's commitment to building trust and transparency through feedback created a more inclusive and supportive work environment, driving overall organizational success.

TRAINING AND DEVELOPMENT PROGRAMS

Training and development programs are essential for embedding feedback into the organizational culture. These programs equip individuals with the skills and knowledge needed to give and receive feedback effectively, fostering a culture of continuous learning and improvement.

Effective training programs focus on building communication skills, empathy, and emotional intelligence. They enable individuals to navigate difficult conversations and provide feedback in a constructive and supportive manner. They also emphasize the importance of active listening, empathy, and self-awareness in receiving feedback gracefully and using it as a catalyst for growth.

Moreover, training programs should be tailored to the unique needs and challenges of the organization, providing practical strategies and tools for integrating feedback into daily interactions and decision-making processes.

TOOLS FOR LEADERS

Training and Development Program: Mastering Feedback for Organizational Growth

Objective: To equip employees with the skills and knowledge needed to give and receive feedback effectively, fostering a culture of continuous learning and improvement.

Duration: 6 months (divided into monthly modules)

Participants: All employees, with tailored sessions for different levels (e.g., entry-level, mid-management, senior leadership)

Program Structure

Month 1: Introduction to Feedback Culture

Week 1: Understanding Feedback

- Workshop: Introduction to the importance of feedback in organizational growth.

- Activity: Group discussions on personal experiences with feedback.

- Outcome: Participants understand the value of feedback and begin to see it as an opportunity for growth rather than criticism.

Week 2: Types of Feedback

- Lecture: Explanation of formal vs. informal feedback and real-time vs. delayed feedback.

- Activity: Role-playing exercises to illustrate different feedback scenarios.

- Outcome: Participants can differentiate between types of feedback and understand when and how to use each.

Week 3: Feedback Models and Frameworks

- Workshop: Introduction to SBI (Situation-Behavior-Impact) and COIN (Context-Observation-Impact-Next steps) models.

- Activity: Practicing using these models in simulated feedback situations.

- Outcome: Participants learn structured approaches to giving feedback.

Week 4: Self-Assessment

- Exercise: Self-assessment of current feedback skills and areas for improvement.

- Outcome: Participants have a clear understanding of their baseline skills and areas to focus on.

Month 2: Building Communication Skills

Week 1: Effective Communication Techniques

- Workshop: Training on clear and concise communication.

- Activity: Group exercises on crafting clear messages and avoiding misunderstandings.

- Outcome: Participants improve their ability to communicate feedback clearly and effectively.

Week 2: Active Listening

- Lecture: Importance of active listening in the feedback process.

- Activity: Listening exercises where participants practice summarizing and reflecting back what they heard.

- Outcome: Participants develop stronger active listening skills.

Week 3: Non-Verbal Communication

- Workshop: Understanding the role of body language and tone of voice in feedback.

- Activity: Pair activities to practice delivering feedback with positive body language and tone.

- Outcome: Participants become more aware of their non-verbal cues and how they affect feedback delivery.

Week 4: Empathy in Communication

- Lecture: The role of empathy in effective communication and feedback.

- Activity: Empathy exercises, including perspective-taking and empathetic listening.

- Outcome: Participants enhance their ability to give and receive feedback empathetically.

Month 3: Emotional Intelligence

Week 1: Introduction to Emotional Intelligence

- Workshop: Overview of emotional intelligence and its components.

- Activity: Self-assessment of emotional intelligence.

- Outcome: Participants understand the basics of emotional intelligence and its importance in feedback.

Week 2: Self-Awareness and Self-Regulation

- Lecture: Techniques for improving self-awareness and self-regulation.

- Activity: Journaling and mindfulness exercises.

- Outcome: Participants become more self-aware and learn to manage their emotions during feedback interactions.

Week 3: Social Skills and Relationship Management

- Workshop: Building social skills for better workplace relationships.

- Activity: Group activities focused on conflict resolution and collaboration.

- Outcome: Participants improve their social skills and learn to manage relationships more effectively.

Week 4: Applying Emotional Intelligence to Feedback

- Exercise: Practicing giving and receiving feedback using emotional intelligence.

- Activity: Real-world scenarios and role-playing exercises.

- Outcome: Participants integrate emotional intelligence into their feedback practices.

Month 4: Navigating Difficult Conversations

Week 1: Preparing for Difficult Conversations

- Workshop: Strategies for preparing for difficult feedback conversations.

- Activity: Planning and rehearsal exercises.

- Outcome: Participants feel more confident and prepared for challenging feedback situations.

Week 2: Delivering Difficult Feedback

- Lecture: Techniques for delivering difficult feedback constructively.

- Activity: Role-playing difficult feedback scenarios.

- Outcome: Participants learn to deliver tough feedback with tact and respect.

Week 3: Receiving Difficult Feedback

- Workshop: Handling negative feedback without becoming defensive.

- Activity: Exercises in receiving and processing difficult feedback.

- Outcome: Participants become more resilient and open to receiving challenging feedback.

Week 4: Follow-Up and Continuous Improvement

- Lecture: Importance of follow-up and continuous improvement after feedback.

- Activity: Creating personal action plans for ongoing development.

- Outcome: Participants commit to continuous learning and improvement based on feedback.

Month 5: Integrating Feedback into Daily Interactions

Week 1: Embedding Feedback in Team Meetings

- Workshop: Techniques for incorporating feedback into regular team meetings.

- Activity: Simulated team meetings with built-in feedback sessions.

- Outcome: Teams learn to make feedback a regular part of their interactions.

Week 2: Creating a Feedback-Rich Environment

- Lecture: Strategies for fostering a culture that encourages ongoing feedback.

- Activity: Group brainstorming sessions on creating a supportive feedback environment.
- Outcome: Participants develop ideas for promoting a feedback culture in their teams.

Week 3: Feedback and Decision-Making

- Workshop: Using feedback to inform decision-making processes.
- Activity: Case studies and role-playing decision-making scenarios with feedback integration.
- Outcome: Participants learn to use feedback to make better-informed decisions.

Week 4: Leveraging Technology for Feedback

- Lecture: Tools and platforms for facilitating feedback (e.g., 360-degree feedback tools, real-time feedback apps).
- Activity: Hands-on training with feedback technology.
- Outcome: Participants become proficient in using technology to enhance feedback practices.

Month 6: Customizing Feedback Practices

Week 1: Tailoring Feedback to Individual Needs

- Workshop: Adapting feedback approaches to suit individual preferences and cultural differences.
- Activity: Developing customized feedback plans for team members.
- Outcome: Participants learn to personalize their feedback approach.

Week 2: Building Feedback into Performance Reviews

- Lecture: Integrating feedback into formal performance review processes.
- Activity: Simulated performance review sessions.
- Outcome: Participants understand how to conduct comprehensive and effective performance reviews.

Week 3: Continuous Learning and Development

- Workshop: Creating ongoing development plans based on feedback.

- Activity: Setting long-term goals and identifying resources for continuous learning.

- Outcome: Participants develop long-term personal and professional development plans.

Week 4: Feedback Culture Celebration

- Event: Celebrating the journey and achievements in feedback culture.

- Activity: Sharing success stories, lessons learned, and future goals.

- Outcome: Participants feel a sense of accomplishment and motivation to continue fostering a feedback-rich environment.

Evaluation and Follow-Up

- Post-Program Survey:

- Collect feedback from participants on the effectiveness of the training program.

Follow-Up Sessions:

- Quarterly check-ins to assess progress and provide additional support.

- Continuous Improvement:

- Use participant feedback to refine and improve the training program for future iterations.

By implementing this comprehensive training and development program, organizations can embed feedback into their culture, equipping employees with the skills and knowledge needed to give and receive feedback effectively, fostering a culture of continuous learning and improvement.

Alternative Training Program: Interactive and Experiential Feedback Mastery

Objective: To foster a culture of feedback by using interactive and experiential learning methods to help employees master the skills of giving and receiving feedback effectively.

Duration: 4 months (divided into bi-weekly modules)

Participants: All employees, with specific sessions tailored for different levels (entry-level, mid-management, senior leadership)

Program Structure

Month 1: Foundations of Feedback

Week 1: Introduction to Feedback Concepts

- Interactive Seminar: Overview of the importance of feedback in personal and organizational growth.

- Activity: Interactive polls and discussions to share initial thoughts on feedback.

- Outcome: Participants understand the critical role feedback plays and recognize common challenges and benefits.

Week 2: Exploring Feedback Models

- Workshop: Deep dive into feedback models like SBI (Situation-Behavior-Impact) and COIN (Context-Observation-Impact-Next steps).

- Activity: Group exercises to apply these models to real-life scenarios.

- Outcome: Participants gain practical experience in using structured feedback models.

Month 2: Communication Skills Development

Week 1: Building Effective Communication Skills

- Interactive Workshop: Techniques for clear, concise communication and avoiding misunderstandings.

- Activity: Small group activities and role-playing to practice communication skills.
- Outcome: Participants enhance their ability to deliver clear, effective feedback.

Week 2: Active Listening and Empathy

- Seminar: Importance of active listening and empathy in feedback.
- Activity: Empathy mapping and active listening exercises in pairs.
- Outcome: Participants develop stronger listening skills and learn to empathize with feedback recipients.

Month 3: Emotional Intelligence and Feedback

Week 1: Emotional Intelligence in the Workplace

- Workshop: Introduction to the components of emotional intelligence.
- Activity: Self-assessment quizzes and group discussions on emotional intelligence.
- Outcome: Participants understand their own emotional intelligence levels and areas for improvement.

Week 2: Applying Emotional Intelligence to Feedback

- Interactive Training: Techniques for using emotional intelligence in feedback situations.
- Activity: Scenario-based role-playing to practice emotionally intelligent feedback.
- Outcome: Participants apply emotional intelligence principles to real feedback situations.

Month 4: Practical Application and Continuous Improvement

Week 1: Feedback in Practice

- Simulation: Real-world feedback scenarios using actors to create lifelike situations.

- Activity: Participants give and receive feedback in simulated environments, followed by group debriefs.

- Outcome: Participants gain confidence in their feedback skills through practical application.

Week 2: Creating a Feedback-Rich Environment

- Workshop: Strategies for embedding feedback into daily work routines and team culture.

- Activity: Group brainstorming sessions to develop actionable plans for fostering a feedback culture.

- Outcome: Participants create tailored plans to integrate feedback into their teams and work processes.

Additional Program Elements

Peer Coaching Circles:

- Bi-weekly Sessions: Small peer groups meet to practice feedback and support each other's growth.

- Activity: Rotating role-play exercises and real-time feedback within the group.

- Outcome: Participants build a supportive network and practice feedback in a safe environment.

Feedback Journals:

- Tool: Participants maintain a feedback journal to reflect on feedback received and given.

- Activity: Weekly prompts guide reflections and action plans based on feedback experiences.

- Outcome: Participants develop self-awareness and track their progress over time.

Digital Learning Platform:

- Resource: Access to online modules, videos, and quizzes to reinforce learning.

- Activity: Self-paced learning with interactive content to complement in-person sessions.

- Outcome: Participants have ongoing access to learning resources and can revisit materials as needed.

Evaluation and Follow-Up

Feedback Assessments:

- Tool: Pre- and post-program assessments to measure improvement in feedback skills.

- Activity: Self-assessment and peer feedback to gauge progress.

- Outcome: Participants see tangible improvements in their feedback skills.

Quarterly Review Sessions:

- Check-In: Quarterly meetings to review progress, share successes, and address challenges.

- Activity: Group discussions and individual presentations on feedback experiences.

- Outcome: Continuous support and reinforcement of feedback culture.

Long-Term Development Plans:

- Tool: Personalized development plans created at the end of the program.

- Activity: One-on-one coaching to develop long-term goals based on feedback received.

- Outcome: Participants leave with a clear roadmap for ongoing personal and professional growth.

By focusing on interactive and experiential learning methods, this training program aims to make feedback a natural and integral part of the organizational culture, ensuring that employees are equipped to give and receive feedback effectively, and fostering continuous learning and improvement.

Continuous Improvement through Feedback Loops

Feedback loops are essential for driving continuous improvement within organizations. They involve regularly collecting, analyzing, and acting on feedback to identify areas for improvement and drive ongoing development.

Effective feedback loops incorporate multiple channels for gathering feedback, including surveys, focus groups, one-on-one meetings, and performance evaluations. They also involve stakeholders at all levels of the organization, ensuring that feedback is comprehensive and representative of diverse perspectives.

Moreover, feedback loops should be accompanied by clear processes for promptly analyzing and acting on feedback. Organizations should establish mechanisms for reviewing feedback, identifying trends and patterns, and developing action plans to address areas for improvement.

By establishing robust feedback loops, organizations can create a culture of continuous improvement in which feedback is valued and used as a catalyst for driving positive change and innovation.

CHAPTER 9

CASE STUDIES & REAL-WORLD APPLICATIONS

This chapter explores real-world examples of how feedback culture has been implemented and its impact on various organizations, educational institutions, and individuals. Through case studies and personal stories, we uncover the transformative power of feedback in driving innovation, fostering growth, and enhancing performance.

Case Study 1: Transforming Organizational Culture at Tech Innovations Inc.

Background: Bite Solutions Inc., a mid-sized technology company, faced challenges with employee engagement and retention. The company's traditional top-down feedback approach left employees feeling undervalued and disconnected, resulting in low morale and high turnover rates.

Implementation: The HR department overhauled the feedback system by introducing a 360-degree feedback approach. This new system encouraged employees at all levels to give and receive feedback from peers, subordinates, and supervisors. The company also conducted workshops on effective communication and feedback, emphasizing the importance of empathy and constructive criticism.

Impact: Employee engagement scores rose by 25% within a year, and turnover rates decreased by 15%. The open feedback culture led to better team collaboration, increased innovation, and a more cohesive work environment. Employees felt more valued and empowered, leading to higher overall performance and job satisfaction. The company also saw an increase in innovative solutions and faster problem-solving as a result of the collaborative atmosphere.

Case Study 2: Enhancing Student Performance at Riverside University

Background: Elite University was struggling with student performance and engagement. Professors primarily provided feedback at the end of the semester, which was too late for students to make meaningful improvements.

Implementation: The university implemented a continuous feedback model where professors provided regular, formative feedback throughout the semester. This included detailed comments on assignments, periodic progress reports, and interactive office hours. Peer review sessions and feedback workshops were also introduced to help students give and receive constructive feedback.

Impact: Student performance improved significantly, with average grades increasing by 10% and course completion rates rising by 20%. The continuous feedback helped students identify their strengths and areas for improvement early, leading to more focused and effective learning. Additionally, student satisfaction with their courses and professors increased, fostering a more supportive and engaging academic environment. Professors also reported feeling more connected to their students, resulting in a more collaborative and interactive learning experience.

Case Study 3: Revitalizing Customer Service at Global Retail Corp

Background: Blue Retail Corp, a multinational retail chain, received frequent customer complaints about poor service quality. The company's feedback culture was hierarchical, and frontline employees rarely received direct feedback from customers.

Implementation: The company launched a customer feedback initiative, allowing customers to provide real-time feedback via mobile apps and in-store kiosks. Frontline employees were trained in receiving and acting on feedback, focusing on empathy and problem-solving. Managers held weekly meetings to discuss customer feedback and implement improvements.

Impact: Customer satisfaction scores improved by 30% within six months. Employees became more proactive in addressing customer needs and resolving issues. The feedback initiative also led to operational changes that streamlined service processes, resulting in faster and more efficient service delivery. The overall customer experience was greatly enhanced, leading to increased loyalty and sales. Employees also felt more connected to their customers, boosting morale and job satisfaction.

Case Study 4: Fostering Innovation at Cree Solutions Agency

Background: Cree Solutions Agency, a marketing and design firm, faced stagnation in creativity and innovation. The company's feedback process was informal and lacked structure, leading to inconsistent and unproductive results.

Implementation: The agency introduced a structured feedback system that included regular brainstorming sessions, peer reviews, and innovation labs. Employees were encouraged to share ideas and provide constructive feedback in a supportive environment. Leadership also established a recognition program to celebrate innovative ideas and successful projects.

Impact: The agency saw a significant boost in creativity and innovation, with a 40% increase in successful project pitches and client satisfaction. The structured feedback system encouraged employees to experiment and take risks, knowing they had the support of their peers and leaders. This shift not only improved the agency's creative output but also enhanced team morale and collaboration. The recognition program further motivated employees to strive for excellence and think outside the box.

Case Study 5: Personal Growth and Leadership Development at Star Consultancy

Background: Star Consultancy, a top-tier consulting firm, aimed to develop its future leaders but faced challenges in providing effective and personalized leadership development.

Implementation: The firm implemented a mentorship program where senior consultants provided ongoing feedback to junior consultants. Leadership workshops and feedback training sessions were introduced. Each junior consultant received a personalized development plan based on feedback from mentors, peers, and clients.

Impact: Junior consultants showed marked improvement in leadership skills and client management, with promotion rates increasing by 35%. The mentorship and feedback culture fostered a sense of continuous learning and development, ensuring a strong leadership pipeline for the future. This also led to better organizational performance and increased impact in their mission-driven work. The personalized development plans helped consultants focus on their individual growth areas, leading to more targeted and effective improvements.

Case Study 6: Increasing Employee Engagement at Healing Medical Center

Background: Healing Medical Center, a large hospital, struggled with low employee engagement and high burnout rates among medical staff—traditional feedback mechanisms needed to be more frequent and often overlooked.

Implementation: The hospital introduced a structured feedback system where medical staff could provide and receive regular feedback through digital platforms and face-to-face meetings. They also implemented "feedback huddles" at the end of shifts for quick, real-time team feedback. To support this initiative, the hospital held workshops on stress management and effective communication.

Impact: Employee engagement scores increased by 20%, and burnout rates decreased by 15% within a year. The regular feedback allowed staff to address issues promptly, share positive experiences, and support each other, leading to a more collaborative and supportive work environment. This also resulted in improved patient care and satisfaction. Staff reported feeling more valued and heard, contributing to a more positive workplace culture.

Case Study 7: Boosting Performance in a Manufacturing Plant

Background: A manufacturing plant faced issues with low productivity and high error rates. The feedback process was top-down, with little input from frontline workers who had valuable insights into operational challenges.

Implementation: The plant introduced a bottom-up feedback system where workers could provide anonymous feedback and suggestions directly to management. Monthly town hall meetings were held to discuss feedback and implement practical solutions. The plant also implemented a suggestion box and a reward system for innovative ideas that improved operations.

Impact: Productivity increased by 25%, and error rates dropped by 30% within six months. The frontline workers felt more valued and involved in decision-making processes, leading to higher job satisfaction and better performance. The collaborative environment also fostered innovation and continuous improvement in plant operations. The reward system motivated employees to contribute ideas, leading to a more dynamic and efficient production process.

Case Study 8: Enhancing Learning in a High School Setting

Background: A high school struggled with student engagement and academic performance. Teachers provided feedback primarily through grades, with little formative feedback to guide students' learning processes.

Implementation: The school implemented a continuous feedback model, where teachers gave regular, formative feedback on assignments and class participation. Peer review sessions and student-teacher conferences were introduced to make feedback more interactive and constructive. The school also incorporated digital tools to facilitate real-time feedback.

Impact: Student engagement and academic performance improved significantly, with average test scores increasing by 15% and graduation rates rising by 10%. The continuous feedback helped students understand their learning progress better and stay motivated. It also fostered a more interactive and supportive learning environment, enhancing the overall educational experience. Teachers reported improved relationships with students and a more dynamic classroom atmosphere.

Case Study 9: Cultivating Leadership at a Non-Profit Organization

Background: A non-profit organization faced challenges with leadership development and succession planning. Feedback was sporadic and needed more depth for meaningful personal growth.

Implementation: The organization introduced a comprehensive feedback and mentorship program. Senior leaders provided ongoing feedback and coaching to emerging leaders, and leadership development workshops were held regularly. The program also included 360-degree feedback to give a well-rounded view of each leader's strengths and areas for improvement.

Impact: The organization saw a significant improvement in leadership capabilities, with many emerging leaders taking on more responsibilities and excelling in their roles. The mentorship and feedback culture fostered a sense of continuous learning and development, ensuring a strong leadership pipeline for the future. This also led to better organizational performance and increased impact in their mission-driven work. The 360-degree feedback provided a holistic view of leadership performance, enabling more targeted development.

Case Study 10: Improving Team Collaboration in a Software Development Firm

Background: A software development firm struggled with poor team collaboration and communication issues, which affected project delivery timelines and quality.

Implementation: The firm adopted agile methodologies, including regular feedback loops such as daily stand-ups, sprint reviews, and retrospectives. Teams were encouraged to give and receive feedback frequently to identify and resolve issues quickly. The firm also provided training on agile practices and effective communication.

Impact: Team collaboration and communication improved dramatically, leading to a 30% reduction in project delivery times and a 25% increase in project quality. The regular feedback loops helped teams stay aligned, address challenges promptly, and continuously improve their processes. This agile feedback culture fostered a more dynamic and responsive work environment, driving better results and higher client satisfaction. The training sessions ensured that all team members were on the same page regarding agile practices, enhancing overall team effectiveness.

These expanded case studies illustrate the transformative power of feedback in various contexts. Whether improving employee engagement, boosting performance, enhancing learning, cultivating leadership, or improving team collaboration, feedback is a critical tool for driving innovation, fostering growth, and enhancing performance across organizations and educational institutions. By embracing a culture of feedback, organizations can create environments where individuals and teams thrive, leading to sustained success and development.

SUCCESSFUL COMPANIES WITH STRONG FEEDBACK CULTURES

Companies like Google, Netflix, and Adobe are renowned for their strong feedback cultures, which are pivotal in driving innovation and performance. At Google, for example, employees are encouraged to give and receive feedback regularly through tools like "Googlegeist" surveys and peer feedback mechanisms. This culture of openness and transparency fosters collaboration, creativity, and continuous improvement, enabling Google to maintain its position as a leader in the tech industry.

Similarly, Netflix emphasizes a culture of radical candor, where employees are expected to provide honest and direct feedback to their peers and leaders. This feedback-centric culture enables Netflix to adapt quickly to changing market dynamics, innovate rapidly, and deliver exceptional customer experiences.

Adobe is another example of a company with a strong feedback culture. Employees are empowered to share their ideas, challenge the status quo, and provide feedback openly and constructively. This culture of feedback has fueled Adobe's growth and success, enabling the company to stay ahead of the curve in a highly competitive industry.

EDUCATIONAL INSTITUTIONS EMBRACING FEEDBACK

Educational institutions increasingly recognize feedback's importance in enhancing learning outcomes and student development. For example, a particular high school in California have implemented feedback-rich environments where students receive regular feedback from teachers, peers, and mentors. This feedback-centric approach to education fosters a culture of collaboration, critical thinking, and continuous improvement, enabling students to thrive academically and personally.

Similarly, universities like Stanford and Harvard have embraced feedback as a core component of their educational philosophy, incorporating feedback mechanisms into their curriculum and pedagogy. By providing students with regular opportunities for reflection, self-assessment, and feedback, these institutions empower students to take ownership of their learning and develop the skills they need to succeed in a rapidly changing world.

PERSONAL STORIES OF TRANSFORMATION THROUGH FEEDBACK

Personal stories highlight the transformative power of feedback in driving significant personal and professional growth. For example, individuals may share stories of how constructive feedback from a mentor or colleague helped them overcome challenges, develop new skills, and achieve their goals. These stories illustrate how feedback can serve as a catalyst for self-reflection, learning, and growth, empowering individuals to reach their full potential.

COACHING CORNER

Story 1: From Struggling Newcomer to Team Leader

Background: a recent graduate, Ann started her first job as a marketing assistant. Eager to make a good impression, she often took on too much work and struggled to meet deadlines.

Feedback and Transformation: Ann's manager, noticing her struggles, provided constructive feedback. He pointed out her enthusiasm but highlighted the need to manage her workload better. He suggested she prioritize tasks and delegate when possible. With this feedback, Ann began using project management tools and learned to delegate tasks effectively. Over time, she became more organized, improved productivity, and was eventually promoted to a team leader position. Ann credits her manager's feedback for helping her develop essential skills and achieve her professional goals.

Story 2: Turning Public Speaking Fears into Strengths

Background: Bert, a talented software developer, was terrified of public speaking. This fear prevented him from presenting his ideas in meetings and conferences.

Feedback and Transformation: Bert's mentor provided feedback on his hesitance to speak publicly during a performance review. She encouraged him to join a public speaking workshop and practice regularly. Initially resistant, Bert decided to confront his fear. He joined a local Toastmasters club and started practicing his presentations. Bert's confidence grew with consistent feedback and support from his mentor and peers. He now speaks at industry conferences and leads workshops, turning his greatest fear into one of his strengths. Bert's transformation showcases the power of feedback in personal development.

Story 3: From Micromanager to Empowering Leader

Background: Lula, a newly appointed project manager, struggled with micromanaging her team. Her need for control led to low team morale and stifled creativity.

Feedback and Transformation: During a feedback session, a colleague gently pointed out Lula's micromanaging tendencies and their impact on the team. Initially defensive, Lula took time to reflect on the feedback. She decided to trust her team more and give them the autonomy to make decisions. Lula focused on clear communication and set expectations while allowing her team the freedom to innovate. As a result, team morale improved, creativity flourished, and projects were completed more efficiently. Lula's journey from micromanager to empowering leader highlights how feedback can drive significant leadership growth.

Story 4: Overcoming Communication Barriers

Background: Mira, an engineer in a multinational company, struggled with communication due to language barriers. Her ideas often went unheard, and she felt isolated from her team.

Feedback and Transformation: A supportive colleague provided feedback on Mira's communication challenges and suggested enrolling in a business English course and joining team-building activities. Mira took this advice seriously. She improved her language skills and actively participated in team events. Over time, her confidence grew, and she started contributing more effectively in meetings. Her innovative ideas were finally recognized, leading to a promotion. Mira's story illustrates how feedback can help overcome personal challenges and unlock potential.

Story 5: Rediscovering Passion through Feedback

Background: Tim, a mid-career professional, felt stuck in his role as a sales manager. His performance had plateaued, and he lost passion for his work.

Feedback and Transformation: During a coaching session, Tim's coach provided candid feedback about his lack of engagement and its impact on his team. She suggested exploring new approaches and setting personal goals aligned with his interests. Tom took a step back to reflect and decided to pursue a certification in digital marketing, an area he had always been curious about. With newfound knowledge and enthusiasm, Tim introduced innovative sales strategies, significantly boosting sales performance. His renewed passion revitalized his career and inspired his team. Tim's experience demonstrates how feedback can reignite passion and drive professional growth.

Story 6: Navigating Conflict Resolution

Background: Ethan, a senior account manager, often found himself in conflicts with team members due to his direct communication style. His bluntness, though well-intentioned, often led to misunderstandings and tension.

Feedback and Transformation: During a company-wide training on effective communication, Ethan received feedback highlighting the need to adopt a more empathetic approach. Encouraged to develop his emotional intelligence, Ethan enrolled in a conflict resolution workshop. He learned to listen actively and approach conflicts with empathy and understanding. Over time, Ethan's relationships with his colleagues improved, and he became known for his ability to mediate and resolve conflicts effectively. Ethan's transformation showcases how feedback can lead to better interpersonal skills and a more harmonious work environment.

Story 7: Building Confidence in Leadership

Background: Grace, a skilled IT professional, was promoted to a leadership position but struggled with self-doubt. She often second-guessed her decisions and hesitated to assert herself in meetings.

Feedback and Transformation: Grace's mentor observed her lack of confidence and provided constructive feedback. He encouraged her to recognize her achievements and strengths and suggested leadership development programs. Grace enrolled in a leadership course and participated in confidence-building exercises. She also sought feedback from her team, which helped her realize her value as a leader. Grace's confidence grew, and she began leading her team with assurance and clarity. Her story highlights the impact of feedback in building self-confidence and effective leadership skills.

Story 8: Enhancing Time Management Skills

Background: Mike, a creative director, struggled with time management. His creative process often led to missed deadlines and last-minute rushes, affecting the team's overall productivity.

Feedback and Transformation: During a performance review, Mike's supervisor provided feedback on the need for better time management. She recommended time management workshops and tools to help him organize his tasks. Mike adopted techniques like time-blocking and prioritization and used project management software to keep track of deadlines. With improved time management skills, Mike's productivity increased, and his team's efficiency improved significantly. Mike's journey underscores how feedback can develop practical skills and enhance productivity.

Story 9: Overcoming Fear of Criticism

Background: Emily, a junior designer, had a fear of criticism that prevented her from sharing her creative ideas. She often kept to herself, missing out on opportunities to contribute to projects.

Feedback and Transformation: Emily's team leader noticed her reluctance to share ideas and provided gentle feedback, encouraging her to view criticism as a tool for growth rather than a personal attack. Emily started actively seeking feedback and gradually became more open to constructive criticism. She practiced presenting her ideas in smaller groups before moving to larger meetings. Emily began contributing more actively as her confidence grew, leading to innovative project outcomes. Her story highlights how feedback can help individuals overcome personal fears and unlock their creative potential.

Story 10: Improving Customer Service Skills

Background: Nikko, a customer service representative, received complaints about his lack of empathy and poor problem-solving skills. His interactions with customers often left them dissatisfied.

Feedback and Transformation: Nikko's supervisor provided detailed feedback, pointing out specific instances where he could have handled situations better. She recommended customer service training focused on empathy and effective communication. Nikko took the training seriously and practiced active listening and empathetic responses. Over time, his customer interactions improved, leading to higher satisfaction scores and fewer complaints. Nikko's transformation illustrates how targeted feedback can significantly improve customer service skills and job performance.

These stories exemplify the transformative power of feedback in personal and professional development. Whether overcoming challenges, developing new skills, or reigniting passion, feedback serves as a catalyst for self-reflection, learning, and growth, empowering individuals to reach their full potential.

LESSONS LEARNED FROM FAILURE AND FEEDBACK

Lessons from failures demonstrate how feedback can turn setbacks into opportunities for learning and improvement. For example, individuals may share stories of how feedback from a failed project or initiative helped them identify areas for improvement, refine their approach, and ultimately achieve success. These stories highlight the importance of embracing feedback as a tool for continuous learning and improvement, even in the face of failure.

Overall, these case studies and personal stories illustrate the profound impact of feedback culture in driving innovation, enhancing performance, and fostering growth across various organizations, educational institutions, and individuals. By embracing feedback as a catalyst for change and growth, organizations and individuals can unlock their full potential and succeed in today's dynamic and rapidly evolving world.

CHAPTER 10

NURTURING GROWTH THROUGH FEEDBACK & MENTORSHIP

In the dynamic landscape of professional growth, feedback and mentorship serve as invaluable compasses, guiding junior-level professionals toward excellence. This chapter delves into the profound significance of constructive insights, the art of seeking feedback, and the pivotal role of mentors in shaping careers.

Understanding the Value of Feedback

Imagine Ella, a diligent junior marketer, meticulously crafting a campaign proposal. Upon submission, she eagerly awaits feedback from her supervisor. Constructive insights arrive, highlighting areas for improvement and commendations for her creativity. With each, Ella hones her skills, gradually transforming into a seasoned marketer.

Feedback, whether positive or an opportunity, fuels professional evolution. This offers a fresh perspective, uncovers blind spots, and fosters a culture of continuous improvement. For junior professionals like Ella, feedback serves as a catalyst for growth, refining their abilities and nurturing resilience in the face of challenges.

Seeking Feedback with Grace

Asking for feedback can be daunting, yet mastering this art is essential for professional development. Consider James, a budding software developer, seeking insights on his coding techniques. He approaches his team lead with humility, acknowledging his eagerness to learn and improve. Through this humble approach, James not only receives invaluable feedback but also cultivates trust and respect within his team.

When soliciting feedback, authenticity and receptiveness are paramount. Express gratitude for the time and insights offered and demonstrate a willingness to act upon constructive insights. By fostering an open dialogue with mentors and supervisors, junior professionals can leverage feedback as a springboard for growth.

Navigating the Mentorship Landscape

Selecting a mentor is akin to choosing a guiding star in the vast cosmos of professional development. Meet Liza an aspiring financial analyst, navigating the complexities of her career path. Through diligent research and networking, she identifies a seasoned analyst as her mentor, drawn to his expertise and approachability.

When selecting a mentor, compatibility and shared values are fundamental. Seek individuals who inspire and challenge, offering guidance tailored to your aspirations. Whether formal or informal, mentorship relationships thrive on mutual respect and genuine rapport, enriching the journey of junior professionals as they navigate the labyrinth of their careers.

Feedback and mentorship are not mere instruments of guidance but pillars of empowerment for junior-level professionals. By embracing constructive insights, soliciting feedback with grace, and navigating the mentorship landscape with discernment, aspiring professionals can forge pathways to excellence. As they embark on their odyssey of growth, let them remember that in the tapestry of their careers, feedback and mentorship are threads of wisdom, weaving the fabric of success.

Difficult Manager

Meet Adam, a dedicated graphic designer with a passion for creativity and innovation. Despite his talents, Alex finds himself at odds with his manager, Ms. Thompson, whose leadership style is characterized as rude and dismissive.

One day, Adam presents a series of design concepts for a client project, eager to receive feedback and refine his work. However, Ms. Thompson dismisses his ideas with a curt remark, refusing to entertain any suggestions for improvement. Frustrated and disheartened, Adam grapples with the realization that his manager is not receptive to feedback.

In the face of adversity, Adam reflects on his options. He recognizes that confronting Ms. Thompson directly may exacerbate tensions and yield no tangible results. Instead, he decides to adopt a strategic approach to address the situation.

Firstly, Adam seeks guidance from trusted colleagues and mentors within the organization, garnering insights on how to navigate the dynamics of his relationship with Ms. Thompson. Their wisdom empowers him to devise a plan of action grounded in professionalism and diplomacy.

Next, Adam chooses to document his ideas and suggestions meticulously, maintaining a record of his creative process and the rationale behind his design choices. By substantiating his proposals with tangible evidence, he aims to present a compelling case for constructive insights and collaboration.

Armed with preparation and poise, Adam seizes an opportune moment to engage Ms. Thompson in a constructive dialogue. With tact and diplomacy, he communicates his desire for open communication and mutual respect in their professional relationship. He emphasizes the value of feedback as a catalyst for growth and innovation, positioning himself as a proactive and solution-oriented team member.

Despite initial skepticism, Ms. Thompson begins to perceive Adam in a new light, acknowledging his professionalism and commitment to excellence. Gradually, she becomes more receptive to his ideas and feedback, fostering a culture of collaboration and trust within their team.

Through resilience and strategic communication, Adam transcends the limitations of a challenging managerial dynamic, transforming adversity into an opportunity for growth and professional development. In navigating the complexities of his relationship with Ms. Thompson, he emerges as a beacon of resilience and integrity, exemplifying the power of grace under pressure.

The Value of Having a Coach

Meet Jess, a recent graduate embarking on her first job as a junior marketing associate. Eager to make her mark, Jess finds herself navigating the nuances of the corporate world under the guidance of her manager, Mr. Patel, a seasoned professional with a passion for mentoring.

Step 1: Recognizing the **Need for Coaching** during a team meeting, Mr. Patel observes Jess struggling to grasp the intricacies of market analysis. Rather than resorting to harsh criticism, he recognizes the opportunity to provide targeted coaching and support.

Step 2: Establishing **Trust and Open Communication**, Mr. Patel schedules a one-on-one meeting with Jess, creating a safe space for open dialogue and mutual respect. He begins by acknowledging Jess's efforts and contributions, fostering a sense of trust and camaraderie.

Step 3: Identifying **Areas for Improvement** with empathy and clarity, Mr. Patel outlines specific areas where Jess can enhance her skills, focusing on the importance of market research and data analysis in strategic decision-making. He refrains from using harsh feedback, opting instead for constructive guidance tailored to Jess's developmental needs.

Step 4: Providing **Actionable Feedback and Resources**, Mr. Patel offers actionable feedback, sharing concrete examples and resources to support Jess's learning journey. He recommends online courses and tutorials, as well as inviting her to shadow senior team members during client meetings to gain firsthand experience.

Step 5: Encouraging **Growth and Accountability**, Mr. Patel emphasizes the importance of continuous improvement and self-reflection, empowering Jess to take ownership of her professional development. He encourages her to set SMART goals (Specific, Measurable, Achievable, Relevant, Time-bound) and offers ongoing support and encouragement along the way.

Step 6: Celebrating **Progress and Milestones**-- As Jess begins to implement Mr. Patel's feedback and recommendations, her confidence and competence blossom. Mr. Patel acknowledges her progress during team meetings, celebrating her achievements and reinforcing a culture of recognition and appreciation.

Through Mr. Patel's patient guidance and mentorship, Jess not only overcomes her initial challenges but also emerges as a confident and capable marketing professional. Their partnership exemplifies the transformative power of coaching, fostering growth, and resilience in the journey toward career success.

A CAREER ROAD MAP FOR NEW LEADERS

Creating a career roadmap for new leaders involves a strategic and holistic approach to guide their professional growth and development. Here's an original framework tailored to the needs of emerging leaders:

1. *Self-Assessment and Reflection:*

Encourage junior leaders to reflect on their strengths, weaknesses, passions, and career aspirations.

Identify personal and professional values, goals, and priorities to establish a foundation for the roadmap.

2. *Define Long-Term Vision:*

Work with junior leaders to envision their ideal future roles and career trajectories.

Set ambitious yet realistic long-term goals aligned with their aspirations and organizational objectives.

3. *Identify Short-Term Goals:*

Break down the long-term vision into actionable short-term goals and milestones.

Prioritize goals based on their relevance, feasibility, and potential impact on career advancement.

4. *Skill Gap Analysis:*

Conduct a comprehensive assessment of the skills and competencies required to achieve the defined goals.

Identify areas where junior leaders need to develop or enhance their skills, knowledge, and capabilities.

5. *Personal Development Plan:*

Collaboratively create a personalized development plan tailored to the specific needs and objectives of each junior leader.

Include a mix of formal training, informal learning opportunities, mentorship, and on-the-job experiences.

6. *Seek Feedback and Guidance:*

Encourage junior leaders to actively seek feedback from supervisors, peers, mentors, and stakeholders.

Provide guidance and support in interpreting feedback and translating it into actionable insights for growth.

7. *Cultivate Leadership Skills:*

Focus on developing essential leadership skills such as communication, decision-making, emotional intelligence, and resilience.

Provide opportunities for junior leaders to lead projects, teams, and initiatives to practice and refine their leadership abilities.

8. *Build a Support Network:*

Foster connections and networking opportunities within the organization and industry.

Encourage participation in professional associations, networking events, and mentorship programs to expand their support network.

9. *Adaptability and Flexibility:*

Emphasize the importance of adaptability and flexibility in navigating dynamic career paths.

Encourage junior leaders to embrace change, seize opportunities, and learn from setbacks and challenges.

10. *Regular Review and Adjustment:*

Schedule regular check-ins to review progress, reassess goals, and make necessary adjustments to the career roadmap.

Encourage junior leaders to reflect on their experiences, celebrate achievements, and recalibrate their plans as needed.

By following this framework, junior-level leaders can chart a clear and purposeful path toward achieving their career aspirations while continuously growing and evolving as professionals and leaders.

CHAPTER 11:

THE POWER OF CONSTRUCTIVE INSIGHTS

As we move into an increasingly digitized and interconnected world, the feedback landscape is undergoing profound transformations. In this chapter, we explore the future of feedback, examining how technology, emerging trends, and remote work dynamics shape how feedback is delivered and received.

THE FUTURE OF FEEDBACK: EMBRACING CONSTRUCTIVE INSIGHTS

The landscape of the modern workplace is rapidly evolving, with a diverse mix of generations working side by side, each bringing unique perspectives, communication styles, and expectations. As organizations strive to foster inclusive and innovative cultures, traditional feedback methods are increasingly falling short. The future of feedback lies in embracing constructive insights—a more holistic, empathetic, and effective approach. Here's why constructive insights are better suited for a multigenerational workplace:

1. Encouraging Continuous Learning and Growth

Constructive insights promote reflection and self-awareness, encouraging employees to think critically about their actions and behaviors. This approach aligns well with the expectations of younger generations, particularly Millennials and Gen Z, who value continuous learning and personal development. By fostering a culture of ongoing improvement, organizations can attract and retain top talent across all age groups.

2. Fostering Inclusivity and Respect

Respect and inclusivity are paramount in a multigenerational workplace. Constructive insights are delivered through open dialogue and mutual respect, ensuring that all employees feel valued and heard. This approach helps bridge generational gaps, creating a more cohesive and collaborative environment.

Older generations, who may value traditional hierarchies, can appreciate the respect and consideration given through insightful discussions, while younger generations, who often seek flatter structures and inclusivity, will feel more engaged and respected.

3. Adapting to Diverse Communication Styles

Different generations have varying communication preferences. Baby Boomers and Gen X may prefer direct, face-to-face conversations, while Millennials and Gen Z might lean towards digital communication and real-time feedback. Constructive insights can be tailored to fit these diverse communication styles, offering flexibility and personalization that traditional feedback methods lack. This adaptability ensures that feedback is effective and well-received across all age groups.

4. Building Emotional Intelligence and Empathy

Constructive insights require high emotional intelligence and empathy from leaders, as they must understand and consider the individual's perspective and feelings. This approach is particularly beneficial in a multigenerational workplace, where employees may have different emotional needs and responses to feedback. Leaders can build stronger, more trusting relationships with their teams by focusing on empathy and understanding, fostering a supportive and positive work environment.

5. Promoting Long-Term Organizational Success

While traditional feedback often focuses on immediate performance improvements, constructive insights aim for long-term growth and development. This forward-thinking approach aligns with the goals of a multigenerational workforce, where older employees may be focused on legacy and mentorship, and younger employees are looking for career growth and future opportunities. By investing in the holistic development of all employees, organizations can build a more resilient, adaptable, and successful workforce.

6. Encouraging Innovation and Creativity

Constructive insights encourage employees to think critically and explore new ideas, which is essential for fostering innovation and creativity. In a diverse, multigenerational workplace, this approach can harness the unique strengths and perspectives of each generation, leading to more innovative solutions and a competitive edge in the market. By valuing and integrating diverse viewpoints, organizations can drive continuous improvement and stay ahead of industry trends.

As the workplace continues to evolve, traditional feedback methods must also adapt. Constructive insights represent the future of feedback, offering a more empathetic, flexible, and effective approach that meets the needs of a multigenerational workforce. Constructive insights can help organizations build a more cohesive, innovative, and successful workplace for all generations by focusing on long-term growth, fostering inclusivity, and adapting to diverse communication styles.

TECHNOLOGY AND FEEDBACK

Technology is revolutionizing feedback practices, providing new tools and platforms that enhance its accessibility, effectiveness, and impact. Artificial intelligence (AI) and machine learning algorithms are being integrated into feedback systems, enabling organizations to analyze large datasets, identify patterns, and provide scale-based personalized feedback.

Apps and digital platforms are also changing the way feedback is given and received, allowing for real-time feedback, multimedia feedback, and asynchronous communication. These tools facilitate ongoing dialogue between individuals, breaking down barriers of time and space and enabling more frequent and meaningful interactions.

Moreover, virtual reality (VR) and augmented reality (AR) technologies are opening new possibilities for immersive feedback experiences, allowing individuals to simulate real-world scenarios and receive feedback in a highly engaging and interactive manner.

EMERGING TRENDS IN FEEDBACK PRACTICES

Several emerging trends are shaping the future of feedback practices, including continuous feedback, 360-degree feedback, and real-time feedback. Continuous feedback involves providing feedback on an ongoing basis, rather than through annual performance reviews, enabling individuals to receive timely and actionable insights into their performance and development.

360-degree feedback, on the other hand, involves soliciting feedback from multiple sources, including peers, managers, and direct reports, providing individuals with a comprehensive view of their strengths and areas for improvement from diverse perspectives.

Real-time feedback emphasizes the importance of providing feedback as soon as possible rather than waiting for formal review cycles. This trend promotes agility, responsiveness, and continuous learning, enabling individuals to course-correct and adapt quickly to changing circumstances.

THE EVOLVING ROLE OF FEEDBACK IN A REMOTE WORK WORLD

The shift towards remote work has changed the feedback dynamics, requiring organizations to adapt their feedback practices to virtual environments. Remote work challenges traditional modes of feedback delivery, such as in-person meetings and face-to-face interactions, necessitating the use of digital tools and platforms for communication and collaboration.

Adapting feedback practices to remote work environments requires a focus on clarity, empathy, and intentionality. Clear communication channels, regular check-ins, and virtual feedback sessions are essential for maintaining connection and performance in remote teams.

Moreover, remote work presents opportunities for leveraging technology to enhance feedback practices, such as using video conferencing for virtual feedback sessions, collaborative platforms for sharing feedback asynchronously, and AI-driven tools for analyzing communication patterns and providing insights into team dynamics.

In conclusion, the future of feedback is characterized by innovation, adaptability, and integration with technology. By embracing emerging trends and leveraging digital tools and platforms, organizations can create feedback cultures that drive continuous improvement, foster collaboration, and empower individuals to thrive in the digital age.

CONCLUSION

RECAP OF KEY POINTS

In this book, we have explored feedback comprehensively, uncovering its psychological foundations, diverse forms, effective techniques, and real-world applications. We've delved into how feedback influences cognition, emotion, and behavior, highlighting the mechanisms through which it shapes our actions and drives growth. We have examined various types of feedback, from praise to constructive criticism, and introduced the concept of constructive insights as the future of feedback—offering deeper understanding and context to foster continuous improvement and innovation.

We've discussed the art and science of giving and receiving feedback, providing practical strategies and frameworks to enhance communication and ensure that feedback is clear, specific, and actionable. We have also addressed challenges and misconceptions surrounding feedback, equipping readers with tools to overcome obstacles and embrace feedback as a catalyst for change. Through insightful case studies and real-world examples, we have illustrated the transformative power of feedback across different contexts, from educational settings to corporate environments.

FINAL THOUGHTS ON THE POWER OF FEEDBACK

Feedback is more than just a transactional exchange of information; it operates on a profound psychological level, shaping our behaviors, motivations, and self-perceptions. Its transformative power lies in its ability to drive growth and development, fostering a culture of continuous improvement. By understanding the intricacies of feedback, we can harness its potential to unlock personal and professional growth, enhance performance, and foster meaningful connections. Whether in the classroom, the boardroom, or personal relationships, feedback is a vital tool for learning and improvement, paving the way for success and fulfillment.

ENCOURAGEMENT FOR THE READER'S FEEDBACK JOURNEY

As we conclude, I encourage you to embrace feedback as a continuous improvement tool and cultivate a positive feedback culture in your own life. Approach feedback with an open mind and a growth mindset, seeing it as an opportunity to learn and grow. Foster an environment where feedback is valued and sought after, where open communication and mutual respect are the norms. By doing so, you will not only enhance your own development but also contribute to the growth and success of those around you. Remember, feedback is a journey—embrace it, learn from it, and let it drive you toward excellence.

COACHING CORNER

FEEDBACK SCRIPTS
FOR LEADERS

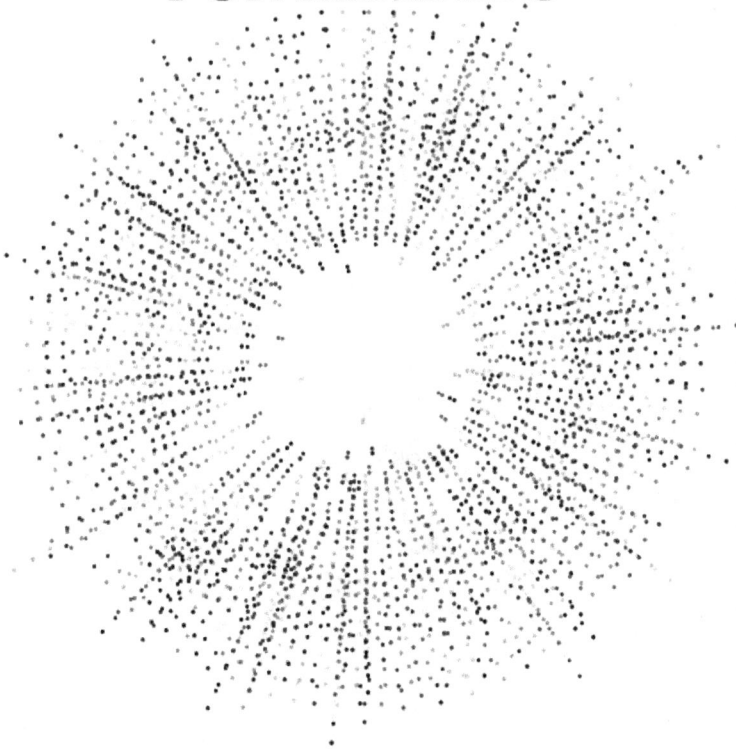

MANAGER PROVIDING FEEDBACK TO EMPLOYEE

Script 1: Praise for Outstanding Performance

Step 1: Manager initiates the conversation.

Manager: "Hi John, can we have a quick chat? I want to discuss your recent project."

Step 2: Manager provides specific feedback.

Manager: "John, I was impressed with how you handled the XYZ project. Your attention to detail and commitment to meeting the deadline were exceptional."

Step 3: Employee responds.

John: "Thank you! I worked hard on it, and I appreciate the recognition."

Step 4: Manager offers further encouragement.

Manager: "Keep up the great work. Your dedication sets a great example for the team. Let's continue to build on this momentum."

Resolution: John feels recognized and motivated to maintain his high performance.

Script 2: Constructive Feedback on Time Management

Step 1: Manager initiates the conversation.

Manager: "Hi, Emily. Could we discuss your recent project timelines?"

Step 2: Manager provides specific feedback.

Manager: "I've noticed that your last two projects were submitted past their deadlines. Can you help me understand what happened?"

Step 3: Employee responds.

Emily: "I've been struggling with balancing multiple tasks and lost track of time."

Step 4: Manager offers constructive insights and solutions.

Manager: "I understand. Let's work on prioritizing your tasks and perhaps use some time management tools to help you keep track. How does that sound?"

Resolution: Emily gains clarity on her time management issues and agrees to use new tools to improve.

Script 3: Addressing a Behavioral Issue

Step 1: Manager initiates the conversation.

Manager: "Hi Mike, do you have a moment to talk about something I've noticed?"

Step 2: Manager provides specific feedback.

Manager: "During meetings, I've observed that you often interrupt others. It can disrupt the flow and make others hesitant to share their ideas."

Step 3: Employee responds.

Mike: "I didn't realize I was doing that. I get excited about the topics."

Step 4: Manager offers constructive insights and solutions.

Manager: "I understand your enthusiasm. Let's work on actively listening and allowing others to finish before you jump in. It will help the team collaborate more effectively."

Resolution: Mike becomes more aware of his behavior and agrees to practice better listening skills.

Script 4: Encouraging Professional Development

Step 1: Manager initiates the conversation.

Manager: "Hi, Sarah. Can we talk about your career development?"

Step 2: Manager provides specific feedback.

Manager: "You've shown great potential in your current role. Have you thought about pursuing any additional training or certifications?"

Step 3: Employee responds.

Sarah: "I have, but I'm not sure where to start."

Step 4: Manager offers constructive insights and solutions.

Manager: "Let's explore some options together. I recommend some courses that align with your interests and career goals."

Resolution: Sarah feels supported in her professional growth and is motivated to further develop.

Script 5: Feedback on Team Collaboration

Step 1: Manager initiates the conversation.

Manager: "Hi Alex, can we discuss your recent collaboration on the team project?"

Step 2: Manager provides specific feedback.

Manager: "I noticed you took charge of the project, which is great, but some team members felt their input wasn't considered."

Step 3: Employee responds.

Alex: "I thought I was helping by leading the way."

Step 4: Manager offers constructive insights and solutions.

Manager: "Leadership is important, but involving everyone is crucial. Let's focus on encouraging more team input in future projects."

Resolution: Alex understands the need for balanced leadership and commits to more inclusive team collaboration.

Script 6: Addressing Performance Issues

Step 1: Manager initiates the conversation.

Manager: "Hi James, can we discuss your recent performance metrics?"

Step 2: Manager provides specific feedback.

Manager: "I've noticed a decline in your sales numbers over the past few months. What challenges are you facing?"

Step 3: Employee responds.

James: "I've been struggling to meet new client targets."

Step 4: Manager offers constructive insights and solutions.

Manager: "Let's analyze your approach and see if we can identify areas for improvement. I can also pair you with a mentor to help you refine your strategies."

Resolution: James agrees to work with a mentor and re-evaluate his sales approach to improve his performance.

Script 7: Recognizing Initiative

Step 1: Manager initiates the conversation.

Manager: "Hi Laura, I wanted to talk to you about your recent initiative on the new marketing strategy."

Step 2: Manager provides specific feedback.

Manager: "Your proactive approach in developing the new strategy was impressive and has been well-received by the team."

Step 3: Employee responds.

Laura: "Thank you! I'm glad it's making a positive impact."

Step 4: Manager offers further encouragement.

Manager: "Keep bringing your ideas forward. Your initiative is valuable and helps drive our success."

Resolution: Laura feels appreciated and encouraged to continue contributing innovative ideas.

Script 8: Providing Feedback on Customer Interaction

Step 1: Manager initiates the conversation.

Manager: "Hi David, can we discuss your recent customer interactions?"

Step 2: Manager provides specific feedback.

Manager: "I've received feedback from a few customers about your helpfulness and professionalism. Great job!"

Step 3: Employee responds.

David: "Thanks! I always try to give my best to our customers."

Step 4: Manager offers further encouragement.

Manager: "Your efforts are noticed and appreciated. Keep up the excellent work and continue to set a high standard for customer service."

Resolution: David feels recognized for his efforts and motivated to maintain his high level of customer service.

Script 9: Addressing Missed Deadlines

Step 1: Manager initiates the conversation.

Manager: "Hi Rachel, can we talk about your recent project deadlines?"

Step 2: Manager provides specific feedback.

Manager: "I've noticed you've missed a few deadlines recently. Is there something affecting your ability to meet them?"

Step 3: Employee responds.

Rachel: "I've been struggling with managing multiple projects at once."

Step 4: Manager offers constructive insights and solutions.

Manager: "Let's review your workload and prioritize your tasks. We can also discuss whether any additional support is needed."

Resolution: Rachel agrees to re-prioritize her tasks and seek additional support if needed, aiming to improve her deadline management.

Script 10: Encouraging Engagement in Team Meetings

Step 1: Manager initiates the conversation.

Manager: "Hi, Tom. Can we talk about your participation in team meetings?"

Step 2: Manager provides specific feedback.

Manager: "I've noticed you're often quiet during meetings. We value your input and would like to hear more from you."

Step 3: Employee responds.

Tom: "I usually listen and process the information before speaking."

Step 4: Manager offers constructive insights and solutions.

Manager: "Your listening skills are valuable, but sharing your thoughts during the meeting can help us make more informed decisions. Maybe you could start by preparing some points beforehand?"

Resolution: Tom agrees to prepare more actively for meetings and share his insights, enhancing team discussions.

Script 11: Feedback on Professional Attitude

Step 1: Manager initiates the conversation.

Manager: "Hi Anita, can we discuss your interactions with colleagues?"

Step 2: Manager provides specific feedback.

Manager: "I've received feedback that your professional attitude and willingness to help others are greatly appreciated."

Step 3: Employee responds.

Anita: "Thank you! I try to support my colleagues as much as I can."

Step 4: Manager offers further encouragement.

Manager: "Your attitude contributes to a positive work environment. Keep up the good work and continue to set a great example."

Resolution: Anita feels recognized for her positive attitude and is motivated to continue supporting her colleagues.

Script 12: Providing Feedback on Technical Skills

Step 1: Manager initiates the conversation.

Manager: "Hi, Kevin. Can we talk about your recent technical performance?"

Step 2: Manager provides specific feedback.

Manager: "Your technical skills have improved significantly, especially in handling complex issues."

Step 3: Employee responds.

Kevin: "I've been working hard to enhance my skills. I appreciate the recognition."

Step 4: Manager offers further encouragement.

Manager: "Great job! Let's discuss opportunities to take on more challenging tasks to continue your growth."

Resolution: Kevin feels acknowledged for his efforts and is motivated to take on more complex tasks to develop his skills further.

Manager Receiving Feedback from Staff

LEADERS SEEKING FEEDBACK

Script 1: General Feedback

Step 1: Manager initiates the conversation.

Manager: "Hi, team. I'd like some feedback on my leadership style. How can I better support you?"

Step 2: Employee provides feedback.

Employee 1: "Sometimes it feels like decisions are made without consulting the team."

Step 3: Manager responds.

Manager: "I appreciate the feedback. I'll try to involve the team more in decision-making processes."

Resolution: The manager commits to involving the team more in decisions, fostering a more inclusive leadership style.

Script 2: Feedback on Communication Effectiveness

Step 1: Manager initiates the conversation.

Manager: "I'd like your honest feedback on how I communicate with the team. What can I improve?"

Step 2: Employee provides feedback.

Employee 2: "Sometimes the information we receive is unclear, leading to confusion."

Step 3: Manager responds.

Manager: "Thank you for pointing that out. I'll work on providing clearer and more detailed communication in the future."

Resolution: The manager pledges to improve communication clarity, aiming to reduce confusion and enhance team understanding.

Script 3: Feedback on Meeting Structure

Step 1: Manager initiates the conversation.

Manager: "Can we discuss how our team meetings are structured? I'd like to hear your thoughts."

Step 2: Employee provides feedback.

Employee 3: "Meetings often run too long and sometimes go off-topic."

Step 3: Manager responds.

Manager: "I appreciate the feedback. I'll work on keeping meetings more focused and time efficient."

Resolution: The manager agrees to streamline meetings, ensuring they are more productive and time efficient.

Script 4: Feedback on Availability

Step 1: Manager initiates the conversation.

Manager: "I want to be accessible to everyone. How can I improve my availability?"

Step 2: Employee provides feedback.

Employee 4: "Sometimes it's hard to schedule time with you because of your busy calendar."

Step 3: Manager responds.

Manager: "I understand. I'll set aside specific times for open office hours each week so you can reach me more easily."

Resolution: The manager implements open office hours to improve accessibility and support for the team.

Script 5: Feedback on Support and Resources

Step 1: Manager initiates the conversation.

Manager: "I'd like your feedback on the support and resources you receive. Are there areas where I can provide more help?"

Step 2: Employee provides feedback.

Employee 5: "We could use more training on our new software tools."

Step 3: Manager responds.

Manager: "Thank you for letting me know. I'll arrange additional training sessions to ensure everyone is comfortable with the new tools."

Resolution: The manager organizes extra training sessions to enhance the team's proficiency with new software tools.

RECEIVING FEEDBACK FROM STAFF

Example 1: Seeking Feedback on Leadership Style

Step 1: Manager initiates the conversation.

Manager: "Hello, team. I'd like to gather some feedback on my leadership style. How do you perceive my approach to leading the team?"

Step 2: Employee provides feedback.

Employee 1: "I appreciate your openness. Sometimes, it feels like we could benefit from more frequent check-ins to ensure we're aligned on priorities."

Step 3: Manager responds.

Manager: "Thank you for sharing your perspective. I'll make sure to schedule more regular check-ins to keep us aligned and address any concerns promptly."

Resolution: The manager commits to implementing more regular check-ins to enhance alignment and communication within the team, fostering a more supportive leadership style.

Example 2: Feedback on Communication Effectiveness

Step 1: Manager initiates the conversation.

Manager: "I'd like your honest feedback on how I communicate with the team. What can I improve?"

Step 2: Employee provides feedback.

Employee 2: "Sometimes the information we receive is not clear, and it leads to confusion."

Step 3: Manager responds.

Manager: "Thank you for pointing that out. I'll work on providing clearer and more detailed communication in the future."

Resolution: The manager pledges to improve communication clarity, aiming to reduce confusion and enhance team understanding.

Example 3: Feedback on Meeting Structure

Step 1: Manager initiates the conversation.

Manager: "Can we discuss how our team meetings are structured? I'd like to hear your thoughts."

Step 2: Employee provides feedback.

Employee 3: "Meetings often run too long and sometimes go off-topic."

Step 3: Manager responds.

Manager: "I appreciate the feedback. I'll work on keeping meetings more focused and time efficient."

Resolution: The manager agrees to streamline meetings, ensuring they are more productive and time efficient.

Example 4: Feedback on Availability

Step 1: Manager initiates the conversation.

Manager: "I want to make sure I'm accessible to everyone. How can I improve my availability?"

Step 2: Employee provides feedback.

Employee 4: "Sometimes it's hard to schedule time with you because of your busy calendar."

Step 3: Manager responds.

Manager: "I understand. I'll set aside specific times each week for open office hours so you can reach me more easily."

Resolution: The manager implements open office hours to improve accessibility and support for the team.

Example 5: Feedback on Support and Resources

Step 1: Manager initiates the conversation.

Manager: "I'd like your feedback on the support and resources you receive. Are there areas where I can provide more help?"

Step 2: Employee provides feedback.

Employee 5: "We could use more training on our new software tools."

Step 3: Manager responds.

Manager: "Thank you for letting me know. I'll arrange additional training sessions to ensure everyone is comfortable with the new tools."

Resolution: The manager organizes extra training sessions to enhance the team's proficiency with new software tools.

TOP 10 MOST DIFFICULT FEEDBACK TOPICS FOR MANAGERS WITH TALKING POINTS

1. Poor Performance

Talking Points:

Introduction: "Hi [Employee], I want to discuss your recent performance."

Specific Examples: "I've noticed that your last three projects were not completed on time and did not meet our quality standards."

Impact: "This has impacted the team's ability to meet deadlines and maintain our high standards."

Support and Solutions: "Let's identify the challenges you're facing and develop a plan to help you improve your performance."

2. Negative Attitude

Talking Points:

Introduction: "Hi [Employee], can we talk about your interactions with the team?"

Specific Examples: "There have been instances where your comments during meetings have come across as dismissive."

Impact: "This has affected team morale and created a tense working environment."

Support and Solutions: "I'd like to work with you on developing a more positive communication approach. How can we address this together?"

3. Lack of Team Collaboration

Talking Points:

Introduction: "Hi [Employee], I'd like to discuss your role in team projects."

Specific Examples: "It seems you often prefer to work alone and haven't been as engaged in team activities."

Impact: "This has led to some miscommunications and a lack of cohesion in our projects."

Support and Solutions: "Let's find ways to improve your collaboration with the team. Maybe we can start by assigning you a partner on the next project."

4. Consistently Missing Deadlines

Talking Points:

Introduction: "Hi [Employee], can we review your recent project timelines?"

Specific Examples: "I've noticed that you've missed several deadlines over the past few months."

Impact: "This has delayed our project schedules and put extra pressure on your colleagues."

Support and Solutions: "Let's discuss what's causing these delays and how we can help you manage your time better."

5. Poor Customer Service

Talking Points:

Introduction: "Hi [Employee], I'd like to talk about your recent customer interactions."

Specific Examples: "We've received feedback that some customers felt their concerns were not fully addressed."

Impact: "This has affected our customer satisfaction scores and could impact our business relationships."

Support and Solutions: "Let's review some customer service techniques and see where we can improve."

6. Inappropriate Workplace Behavior

Talking Points:

Introduction: "Hi [Employee], I must address a sensitive issue regarding your behavior."

Specific Examples: "There have been reports of unprofessional comments that have made colleagues uncomfortable."

Impact: "This behavior is not aligned with our company values and creates a hostile work environment."

Support and Solutions: "We need to address this immediately. I'm here to support you in understanding and correcting this behavior."

7. Lack of Initiative

Talking Points:

Introduction: "Hi [Employee], I want to discuss your engagement with your work."

Specific Examples: "I've noticed that you haven't been taking the initiative in your projects and often wait for instructions."

Impact: "This has slowed down our progress and limited our ability to innovate."

Support and Solutions: "Let's work on setting clear expectations and finding ways to encourage more proactive behavior."

8. Resistance to Change

Talking Points:

Introduction: "Hi [Employee], can we talk about your response to recent changes in the workplace?"

Specific Examples: "It seems you've been resistant to adopting new processes and tools."

Impact: "This resistance is affecting our ability to adapt and improve our operations."

Support and Solutions: "Let's discuss the concerns you have and how we can support you through this transition."

9. Frequent Absences or Tardiness

Talking Points:

Introduction: "Hi [Employee], I want to discuss your attendance record."

Specific Examples: "You've been frequently late and have missed several days of work recently."

Impact: "This has impacted the team's ability to rely on you and complete tasks on time."

Support and Solutions: "Let's talk about what's causing these absences and how we can address them to improve your attendance."

10. Subpar Quality of Work

Talking Points:

Introduction: "Hi [Employee], can we review the quality of your recent work?"

Specific Examples: "There have been multiple instances where your work did not meet the expected standards."

Impact: "This has required additional time for revisions and affected our project timelines."

Support and Solutions: "Let's identify specific areas for improvement and provide additional training or resources to help you enhance the quality of your work."

MOTIVATING TOPICS FOR STAFF

1. Embracing Change and Innovation

Introduction: "Good morning, team! Today, I want to discuss embracing change and innovation's power."

Motivation: "Change can be daunting, but it also brings opportunities for growth and improvement. Innovation is what drives our progress and keeps us ahead of the competition. Let's approach change with an open mind and see it as a chance to learn and grow."

Action: "Let's commit to being adaptable and creative. Share your big or small ideas, and let's work together to turn them into reality. Remember, every great innovation started with a simple idea."

2. Fostering a Positive Work Environment

Introduction: "Hello, team! I want to take a moment to talk about the importance of fostering a positive work environment."

Motivation: "A positive work environment boosts morale, productivity, and overall job satisfaction. When we support and uplift each other, we create a space where everyone can thrive."

Action: "Let's try to acknowledge each other's contributions, offer help when needed, and maintain a positive attitude. Together, we can build a workplace that we all look forward to coming to every day."

3. Commitment to Excellence

Introduction: "Hi team, I want to discuss our commitment to excellence and how it defines our work."

Motivation: "Excellence isn't about being the best; it's about doing your best. The attention to detail, the dedication to quality, and the drive to continuously improve sets us apart."

Action: "Let's strive for excellence in everything we do. Pay attention to the details, take pride in your work, and always look for ways to improve. Together, we can achieve greatness."

4. The Power of Teamwork

Introduction: "Good afternoon, team! Today, let's talk about the power of teamwork."

Motivation: "Individually, we can achieve a lot, but together, we can achieve so much more. Teamwork combines our strengths and talents, leading to better solutions and greater success."

Action: "Let's collaborate, communicate, and support each other. Celebrate our collective wins and learn from our challenges together. Remember, we are stronger as a team."

5. Encouraging Continuous Learning

Introduction: "Hello, everyone; I want to highlight the importance of continuous learning."

Motivation: "Learning doesn't stop when we leave school. It's a lifelong journey that keeps us adaptable, skilled, and ready for new challenges. By continuously learning, we stay relevant and competitive."

Action: "Let's commit to ongoing personal and professional development. Seek out new knowledge, take advantage of training opportunities, and share what you learn with the team. Our growth as individuals fuels our growth as a company."

6. Recognizing and Celebrating Success

Introduction: "Hi team, let's take a moment to recognize and celebrate our successes."

Motivation: "Recognition boosts morale and motivates us to keep striving for excellence. Celebrating our achievements, no matter how big or small, reminds us of our progress."

Action: "Let's make it a habit to acknowledge and celebrate our wins. Share your accomplishments with the team, and let's take pride in each other's successes. Together, we can create a culture of appreciation and motivation."

7. Building Resilience

Introduction: "Good morning, team! I want to talk about the importance of building resilience."

Motivation: "Resilience is our ability to bounce back from setbacks and keep moving forward. It's what helps us stay focused and motivated, even in challenging times."

Action: "Let's support each other through the tough times and celebrate our resilience. Remember, every challenge is an opportunity to grow stronger. Together, we can overcome any obstacle."

8. Embracing Accountability

Introduction: "Hi, everyone; I want to discuss the importance of accountability."

Motivation: "Accountability means taking responsibility for our actions and their outcomes. It builds trust and respect within the team and ensures we all contribute to our shared goals."

Action: "Let's hold ourselves and each other accountable. Be transparent about your progress, ask for help when needed, and take ownership of your work. Together, we can achieve our goals with integrity."

9. Inspiring Creativity

Introduction: "Hello team, today I want to inspire you to embrace your creativity."

Motivation: "Creativity is the spark that drives innovation and problem-solving. When we think creatively, we find new and better ways to do things."

Action: "Let's create an environment where creativity is encouraged and valued. Share your ideas freely, take risks, and don't be afraid to think outside the box. Together, we can turn creative ideas into innovative solutions."

10. Cultivating a Growth Mindset

Introduction: "Good afternoon, team! Let's talk about cultivating a growth mindset."

Motivation: "A growth mindset is the belief that our abilities can be developed through dedication and hard work. It fosters a love of learning and resilience essential for great accomplishments."

Action: "Let's embrace challenges, learn from feedback, and persist through obstacles. Celebrate effort and progress, not just outcomes. Together, we can achieve incredible things by cultivating a growth mindset."

By incorporating these motivating talks into regular team meetings or individual conversations, leaders can inspire their staff to strive for excellence, foster a positive and collaborative work environment, and continuously grow personally and professionally.

BONUS

CHECKLIST FOR MANAGERS: PROVIDING CONSTRUCTIVE INSIGHTS AS FEEDBACK

Instructions:

This checklist is designed to help managers provide constructive insights as feedback to their employees. Constructive insights go beyond traditional feedback by offering deeper understanding and context, fostering continuous improvement, and encouraging growth. Use this checklist during one-on-one meetings, performance reviews, or any feedback session to ensure your feedback is meaningful, actionable, and supportive.

Pre-Feedback Preparation

- Identify Specific Behaviors or Outcomes:

- Clearly define the specific behavior or outcome you want to address.

- Gather examples or data to support your observations.

Understand the Context:

- Consider the circumstances that may have influenced the employee's behavior or performance.

- Reflect on the employee's overall performance, strengths, and areas for improvement.

Set a Positive Tone:

- Approach the feedback session with a positive and supportive attitude.

- Plan to start the conversation by acknowledging the employee's efforts and contributions.

- During the Feedback Session

Create a Safe Environment:

- Ensure privacy and choose a comfortable setting for the conversation.

- Express your intention to help the employee grow and improve.

- Use the SBI Model (Situation-Behavior-Impact):

Situation: Describe the specific situation where the behavior or outcome occurred.

- Example: "During last week's team meeting…"

- Behavior: Describe the specific behavior or action.

- Example: "I noticed that you interrupted your colleagues' multiple times."

- Impact: Explain the impact of the behavior on the team or project.

- Example: "This disrupted the flow of the meeting and made others hesitant to share their ideas."

Encourage Self-Reflection:

- Ask open-ended questions to encourage the employee to reflect on their behavior.

- Example: "How do you think this behavior affects the team's dynamics?"

- Listen actively and allow the employee to share their perspective.

Provide Constructive Insights:

- Offer specific, actionable insights for improvement.

- Example: "One way to improve team collaboration is to practice active listening. Let's work on allowing others to finish speaking before you share your thoughts."

- Provide context and rationale for your suggestions.

- Example: "Active listening can help create a more inclusive environment and encourage everyone to participate."

Collaborate on Solutions:

- Work together to develop a plan for improvement.

- Example: "Let's set a goal for the next meeting to focus on active listening. I'll also provide you with some resources on effective communication techniques."

- Agree on specific actions and timelines.

- Offer Support and Resources:

- Identify any additional support or resources the employee may need.

- Example: "Would you benefit from a communication workshop or a mentor to help you improve your skills?"

- Reaffirm Your Confidence:

- Express your confidence in the employee's ability to improve and succeed.

- Example: "I believe in your potential to grow in this area and contribute positively to our team. I'm here to support you every step of the way."

- Post-Feedback Follow-Up

Monitor Progress:

- Check in regularly to discuss the employee's progress and provide ongoing support.

- Offer additional feedback and adjust the improvement plan as needed.

Acknowledge Improvements:

- Recognize and celebrate the employee's efforts and achievements.

- Example: "I've noticed significant improvements in your communication during meetings. Great job!"

Reflect and Adjust:

- Reflect on the effectiveness of the feedback session and make adjustments for future feedback interactions.

- Seek feedback from the employee on how the process can be improved.

- Summary

Pre-Feedback Preparation:

- Identify specific behaviors or outcomes.

- Understand the context.

- Set a positive tone.

During the Feedback Session:

- Create a safe environment.

- Use the SBI model.

- Encourage self-reflection.

- Provide constructive insights.

- Collaborate on solutions.

- Offer support and resources.

- Reaffirm your confidence.

Post-Feedback Follow-Up:

- Monitor progress.

- Acknowledge improvements.

- Reflect and adjust.

Using this checklist will help you provide constructive insights that are clear, actionable, and supportive, fostering a culture of continuous improvement and growth within your team.

ABOUT THE AUTHOR

Dr. Tenia Davis is a distinguished authority in the fields of Human Resources and Operational Excellence, with a storied career that includes executive roles at esteemed organizations such as Harpo Productions (The Oprah Winfrey Show), iManage, Johnson Publishing Company, and Raise. With a proven track record of excellence in managing complex practices, standards, and regulations, Dr. Davis has been a driving force in talent acquisition, HR management, and multiple corporate departments.

Presently serving as the Chief People Officer at NORC at the University of Chicago, Dr. Davis leads the People and Diversity Racial Equity, Inclusion (DREI) functions, drawing upon her expertise in change management, organizational development, and diversity initiatives to steer the organization towards success. Her academic credentials include an MBA from Loyola University of Chicago and a Ph.D. from Benedictine University's Center for Values-Driven Leadership. Dr. Davis is not only an accomplished scholar but also a community leader, dedicated to mentoring emerging leaders and giving back to society.

www.ingramcontent.com/pod-product-compliance
Lightning Source LLC
Chambersburg PA
CBHW071415210326
41597CB00020B/3516